Geeta Somjee is a full-time researcher and an international development consultant. She attended the London School of Economics and took her PhD at Baroda University. She has been a Visiting Fellow at Queen Elizabeth House, Oxford, and at Wellesley College Center for Research on Women, and has spent several years doing longitudinal field research in rural and urban India. She is the author of articles in various social science journals and chapters in co-authored books.

NARROWING THE GENDER GAP

Narrowing the Gender Gap

Geeta Somjee

St. Martin's Press   New York

First published in the United States of America in 1989

Printed in Hong Kong

ISBN 0–312–01207–1

Library of Congress Cataloging-in-Publication Data
Somjee, Geeta, 1930–
Narrowing the gender gap / by Geeta Somjee.
p.   cm.
Includes index.
ISBN 0–312–01207–1 : $45.00 (est.)
1. Women—India—Social conditions.   2. Women—India—
Socialization.   3. Sex role—India.   4. India—Social
conditions—1947–   I. Title.
HQ1743.S63 1989
305.4′2′0954—dc19

Dedicated to the memory of my parents

Contents

Preface

This book is about a variety of efforts to help women overcome the constraints and disadvantages imposed on them by the traditional society of India. Such efforts were largely directed against the network of social relationships, attitudes of men, gaps in social policy, specific cultural values, and deeply entrenched social practices which tend to treat women as unequal. The variety of continuing efforts identified in this volume, to question such an inferior status and also to involve women in various regenerative processes to help overcome the gender gap, range from social movements, to specific efforts by the elite, to the involvement of women themselves in various participatory processes of the newly created economic and political institutions. The overall social consequence of such efforts needs to be identified in its actuality. It will be the argument of this book that since Indian society is highly segmented, diverse and hierarchical, its women require a variety of efforts to be able to overcome its traditional gender gap, and that any attempt to think in terms of simple institutional, public policy, economic or legal rights solutions to their problems would not be enough. Much more needs to be done. Since women have lived in a status of secondary importance for far too long, they need self-involvement in participatory social processes to be able to overcome their own deeply internalised notions of inferiority and secondariness. In this volume we shall identify a variety of such efforts in rural and urban India and their effect on the traditional gender gap.

In the present work we shall identify problems of women against their actual social and cultural background. While women can be regarded as a disadvantaged group almost universally, the nature and reason for such a situation, as also for a way out of it, are not the same everywhere. Consequently, those theoretical approaches in scholarly writings on women's studies which ignore this basic fact are of limited value.

Apart from the questionable approach of seeking universal validity for certain therapeutic arguments, based on the historical or contemporary experiences of women in a few western countries, the very practice of theoretical generalisations based on reductionist exercises, wanting to reduce highly complex social reality to what can be managed within the framework of one's simple theories, has not deepened our understanding of the peculiar problems of women in different societies. On the contrary, it has constrained and even distorted our understanding of the complex, unparallel, diverse and internally changing aspects of the social reality of unfamiliar non-western societies.

In no society can "women" be considered to be a monolithic block with a common set of problems. Despite a common gender, a continuing status of disadvantage through the ages, across cultures and historical periods, they and their problems are different. Their problems are further compounded in a society like the Indian with its mind-boggling ethnic plurality and cultural diversity, leading to differentiated responses to development stimulus. And what is more, women in some of those ethnic groups, governed by their own cultural norms, are also registering minute but incremental gains in their drive towards new gender equations, and altering the traditional attitude of their menfolk towards them.

Within the Indian situation we have to deal with not only its complex social and cultural diversity but also its equally complex internal dynamics. We shall, therefore, view the problems of women not only against the background of their social and cultural contexts but also in terms of the minutiae and nuances of their own gains within the network of social relationships.

Unlike the countries of the west, India did not, historically speaking, go through a process of economic and political individuation. Such a process was introduced in the west by the powerful commercial and industrial entrepreneurial drive of liberal capitalism from the seventeenth to the twentieth century. As opposed to that the Indian experience of individualism, which was introduced at the dawn of Indian classical civilisation, remained largely at the level of the pursuit of intellectual and spiritual values. Consequently, unlike the individualised economic and political society of the countries of the west, the Indian experience of associated living and acting, through various ascriptive groups such as family, caste, neighbourhood, village etc., remained, by and large, a part of its continuing experience. Such a legacy of associated living has given to the women of India certain special roles and functions with their own advantages and disadvantages. Any discussion on the problems of Indian women should therefore not overlook the fact that realistically speaking they, as well as men, are integral parts of wider ascriptive social units.

The dynamics of change in gender relationships, and in the attitude of society as a whole towards women, needs to be identified, explained and evaluated in all its significant aspects. One of the important aspects of change is that which occurs during generational successions. In each such succession there are shifts in values and emphases, extensions of domains, demands for new roles, and the questioning of the inherited wisdom.

But the concept of generation within the Indian context will be meaningless unless we use it with reference to the highly segmented and stratified nature of her society. Karl Mannheim, who had done a lot of thinking on the concept, felt that our perspectives on society, as seen through the concepts of ethnicity and class, need to be supplemented by the notions of common or generational imprints which people of different classes and ethnic groups are exposed to. Such an added generational dimension will no doubt enrich our perception of society. Nevertheless, within the Indian situation, and more specifically among her women, as we shall see, only in certain ethnic groups do generational perspectives blur the ethnic division. In the rest they go along the ethnic and religious divide.

But in criss-crossing ethnicity and religion with generation, we shall not overlook the fact that within the traditional society of India various social groups also stand in an emulative relationship with one another. While in cultural matters the emulation is vertical, lower social groups imitating the cultural norms of higher social groups, a process aptly described by M. N. Srinivas as "Sanskritisation", in economic and educational matters the emulation could be of the advancements which the lower half of the traditional society has registered. Such an emulative process, both vertical and horizontal, as we shall see, is also noticeable among women.

The generational analysis of women is not devoid of its own problems. For one thing, because of various modernising exposures, such an analysis was relatively easier in urban communities than in rural. There again different generational distances, shifts, disruptions, and fusions created their own problems of identifying different generations as discrete groups. Consequently, only for the purposes of a nuanced social analysis of the subjective states and thinking of women in various social groups was it undertaken, knowing full well that in the next round of one's interview and analysis one might see a slightly different view or position on the same issue.

The generational analysis of women leaders, as we shall see in the following pages, also revealed some interesting features. The urban women leaders did not come from an unhappy family background nor did they adopt a confrontationist attitude towards men as such. On the contrary, most of them were literally persuaded and pushed into taking initiatives in defence of women's causes by their own enlightened and liberal male relatives, i.e. father, husband or brother. Consequently, in their emphasis on social reform and a fair deal for women, they played down the element of confrontation either against men in general or against male decision-makers. Such an approach helped them to mobilise a much larger mass of women, as the latter saw in women leaders good family women. Even the younger generation of women, with potential for leadership, revered them and went along with their near absence of male hostility.

The prolonged predominant position of the women leaders of the first generation, as is evident in most developing countries, did not allow the succeeding generation of leadership to build itself, not even as apprentices. The older generation of leadership literally subsumed the one next to it. This is a widespread phenomenon in developing countries where the leaders who fight for national independence stay on in power far too long, eating up the opportunity of the following generation to take over. Similarly, the women leaders of the older generation did not leave any scope for the generation immediately following them. How and when a new generation, after the one that is consumed, will gain an entry into the corridors of power still remains to be seen and recorded.

There are several aspects of social relationships and attitudes which consign women to positions of disadvantage. Some of them can be dealt with, in a variety of ways, to create a new social space, as it were, for women to operate in. And cumulatively such creations can begin to make a significant difference to gender relationships. The mobilisation of women in India at the hands of social and religious reformers, and later on by nationalist leaders, together with various institutional provisions and social policies for equality of opportunity and the protection of women,

could go only so far. After that specific attempts in particular
areas were needed to help women overcome the built-in
constraints in the network of social relationships and attitudes
within the traditional society.

The four instances of such specific efforts by urban women
leaders operating in rural and periurban areas, which are
discussed in this volume, addressed themselves to the specifics
of women's problems with a deep sense of what is manageable
and possible. Underlying their efforts there was an assumption
that a part of women's problems, of social disadvantage and
constraint, can be tackled by means of elite mobilisation, and
that such an effort can supplement the work of institution
builders and policy makers. Not only that, but what was needed,
according to them, was to slice away from the gross mass of
women's problems a specific portion for themselves and their
organisation to tackle. Just pick up only as much at a time as
you can make the needed difference to in terms of fresh
opportunity for women to involve themselves in. Such a "piecemeal social engineering", to use Karl Popper's term, proved to
be, as we shall see, highly effective.

None of the efforts by the urban elites, at mobilising women,
would have borne fruit had they not latched them on to economic
organisations of one kind or another in their regions. Nothing
proved to be more effective in mobilising women as an initial
concentration on the economic dimension of their problems. But
such a dimension, as we shall see, was far more complex than
the demand for fair or equal wages. In the shifting social scene,
where demands of a disadvantaged gender were registered and
often responded to with less and less delay, it was always easier
to express them in quantifiable terms. But such demands were
in fact an integral part of the network of social relationships,
cultural values, and attitudes which had led to their articulation
in the first place.

Over and above the provisions of institutions and social policy,
exposure to the forces of modernisation and education, and the
mobilisation of women leaders in specific areas, what helped
women the most in making gains in narrowing down the gender
gap was their own involvement in the economic and political
processes of the newly created institutions with participatory
provisions in their own regions. The more the women involved
themselves in those processes, the greater was their realisation

of their own true worth. But when more and more doors were opening for them, they wanted to balance their entry into the new social space with their own family life, intact, which they deeply cherished. Consequently, in some cases the push for greater involvement in participatory opportunities was abruptly halted, leaving to others the scope for grabbing them if they so wished. Once again the responses of women to the new opportunities, in a segmented, hierarchical and socially unequal society were different. In most cases the deeply established cultural values and attitudes of men determined how far their women would involve themselves in those participatory processes. What is interesting to note here is that the extent of women's involvement did not always correspond with the built-in advantages in their ritual, economic and educational background.

To begin with, women at the top and the bottom of the traditional social organisation registered, for different cultural reasons, much greater drive and ease in involving themselves in the decision-making processes of the newly created institutions. The rationale for such an involvement, at the two ends of the ethnic spectrum, remained different. For the Brahmin women it was, by and large, a traditional rationale of their having a moral obligation, being a caste of teachers and cultural standard-bearers, to set a good example of women's participation for the rest of the community to follow. At the other extreme, women of tribal groups which did not have the traditional gender distance of caste groups, did not have to make a special effort to gain an access to such bodies.

Between those two extremes there were the women of agriculturist castes, in particular, the Patidars. As a rule they had, relatively speaking, a much stronger economic and educational background. But the nature and extent of their social interaction, at least in rural communities, was determined by the notions of respectability as articulated by men. If they thought, as they invariably did, that the respectability of Patidar women would be compromised if the latter rubbed shoulders with men either in the workplace or in public institutions, their womenfolk could not cross those male-imposed boundaries of respectability. Consequently, the Patidar women, who had more education and the leisure to be able to make an effective contribution to public bodies, were kept away from them. Such constraints on their activity was much less in evidence in urban centres. The Patidar women, sometimes recent migrants to urban centres, enjoyed much greater freedom and extent of participation in public institutions with, genderwise, unmixed or mixed composition.

The women of Chaudhury caste, a close variant of the Patidars, revealed yet another pattern of involvement. They were deeply involved in the milk economy of the region and also took an interest in issues relating to it in public bodies. But they did not want to get involved in their decision-making processes. They were content to influence and supervise the activities and positions of their males while the latter made those decisions.

Then there were instances of women of mixed caste groups, largely dominated by the lower castes, who were made decision-makers in economic and political institutions out of the sheer idealism of male leaders. Those leaders believed, as we shall see in this study, that only when women themselves got involved in various economic and political processes and their decision-making bodies, would they be able to grow in their political capacity.

The picture of women's involvement in newly created participatory institutions was thus a varied one. The extent of their involvement continued to be determined by the economic and educational level of both women and men, the cultural values of their groups, the attitude of men towards women, the prevalent notions of respectability, and the extent to which the women themselves wanted to go, given their manifold responsibilities. To all these factors the emulative framework, within which various social groups co-existed, also made some difference.

In this study I have looked at the phenomenon of narrowing the gender gap as a complex, varied, and continuing process. My understanding of it is based on longitudinal field research in rural and urban communities of Gujarat over a period of more than two decades. From 1966 to 1977, I acted as the principal investigator in A. H. Somjee's study *Democratic Process in a Developing Society* (1979). While we were engaged in looking at the actualities of democratic process, I also paid some attention to the involvement of women in it. After that in 1982–3, 1983–4, 1984–5 and 1985–6, I started concentrating on women in rural and urban communities. Apart from the urban communities of Anand and, more recently, of Mehsana, I visited several rural communities in the districts of Kaira, Mehsana, Ahmedabad, Surat, Sabarkantha and Panchmahals, again and again. In this connection I would particularly like to thank my two research assistants: Raksha Patel and Bela Patel.

I benefited a great deal by discussing my research findings and analysis with various scholars. In particular I would like to thank Shirley Ardener and Helen Callaway of the Centre for Cross-Cultural Research on Women at Queen Elizabeth House, Oxford. I would also like to thank Laura Lein, Susan McGee Bailey and Jan Putnam for all their help and encouragement. The two academic years as Visiting Research Scholar in 1983–4 and 1987–8 at the Center for Research on Women at Wellesley College, Wellesley, Massachusetts, immensely helped me in thinking through some of the problems in my research. Finally, I have received, as a large number of scholars of Indian origin have received, constant encouragement and help from the two senior scholars of Indian studies, i.e. Norman Palmer and K. Ishwaran.

The Social Sciences and Humanities Research Council of Canada gave me grants to do field research in India. Without their assistance a work of this nature could not have been undertaken.

I would also like to thank the librarians of the Indian Institute and Queen Elizabeth House, Oxford; Wellesley College; Harvard University; and Simon Fraser University.

This manuscript has gone through several drafts, and my husband, A. H. Somjee, proved to be a constant source of editorial assistance and encouragement. Since we have jointly done field research in urban and rural India for more than two decades, it was not always possible to copyright our respective approaches and ideas.

For whatever shortcomings there are in this volume, I alone am responsible.

West Vancouver   Geeta Somjee

1 Approaches to the Study of Problems of Women

In the history of women's studies, which is not very long, a variety of approaches have been adopted in order to understand women's problems and find solutions to them. Such approaches range from how women are perceived in various cultures and historical settings, given their biological functions and what nature "intended" them to do, to their decline in power and status *vis-à-vis* men in the complex social evolution, to a widely shared emphasis on the need to make women equal through the economic and legal route which treats them as individuals rather than those having the sole responsibility for looking after the family.

All these approaches, as we shall presently see, underline various vital aspects of problems which have plagued women in practically all societies, across cultural conditions and historical periods. What still needs to be emphasised, however, is the baffling plurality and diversity of such problems within any particular society. Such a diversity is often played down by us in order to build our all-embracing theoretical arguments. Moreover, rarely do we get round to questioning the efficacy of the various conceptual tools that we use in order to identify and explain the peculiar problems of women in different societies. Such questions become inevitable when we look at the awesome complexity of Indian society and of the problems of women within it. In this chapter we shall throw light on the need to adopt an approach which shows an awareness of such problems.

The chapter is divided into the following parts: cultural perceptions and role definitions; critics of cultural practices; the institutional approach; the economic approach; and the contextual approach. We shall now examine each of these in some detail.

CULTURAL PERCEPTIONS AND ROLE DEFINITIONS

One of the intractable questions of dealing with the problems of women, as presented in scholarly works and their often universalised theories, is whether or not such problems and their proposed solutions are couched in ethnocentric terms. As a perceptive anthropologist, Shirley Ardener, has remarked, ". . . we tend to think of the category of 'women' as some kind of universal, with a place in cross-cultural reference. We should not be allowed to forget that our own cultural model of women . . . are very special examples from wider category called 'women'." Further, "clearly an English model has no ultimate theoretical or moral primacy. . . ."[1]

A similar concern was expressed by another distinguished anthropologist, namely Scarlett Epstein, about the quality of scholarly writings and the solutions proposed. In her words, "The recent Feminists and Women's Liberation movements are products of Western cultures. Though they are performing a laudable task in stressing the need of integrating women in development programmes, which was first indicated by Boserup (1970), many of their arguments are ethnocentric with applicability to Western culture and frequently only to certain sections of women within developed countries; they bear little, if any, relevance to the lives of most women in less developed countries."[2]

Consequently, to be able to understand women in different cultural groups, we shall have to have some understanding, first of all, of how they are "perceived" in them, together with "ground rules" and "social maps" which such groups provide for women's roles and functions within them.[3]

Such "perceptions", in turn, are shaped by societies' views of the biological properties or natural endowments of "women" and how they, the different societies, can use them.[4] Society's "perceptions", in other words, would lay down certain ground rules for governing women's activities, jurisdictions and relationships.

Such "perceptions" of women, and the ground rules defining their roles and relationships, were crystallised and imposed by certain cultural layers in specific societies and reinforced by references to holy books. That is what happened in the Indian situation. The various *shastras*, the religious and philosophical texts, together with views and commentaries by saints and seers, provided a normative structure for women's place in society. Such a normative structure was further compounded by India's traditional hierarchical social organisation and a prolonged period of social destabilisation spread over nearly eight hundred years of almost continuous foreign invasions and conquests. In her case, therefore, the thick layer of her classical culture, together with historical experiences dictating their own concerns regarding the protection of women, created the bulk of problems for women in India.

The prolonged process of social destabilisation also added to her inability to do anything about those problems. Such a situation reached its climax on the eve of the British entry into India. After that *pax Britannica* provided an opportunity to her social and religious reformers to reflect, write, and mobilise public opinion against a number of self-degrading social practices and customs involving the treatment of women. Women obviously were at the receiving end of the inhuman treatment involved in sutee, purdah, polygamy, child marriages and different forms of prostitution.[5] The thinking and reform-minded individuals felt ashamed of what they, as a people, had done to their womenfolk. The arrogant colonial rulers and the supercilious Christian missionaries also reminded them, in their various ways, that in the ultimate analysis the treatment of women symbolises the quality of a civilisation. Consequently, from the early nineteenth century onwards, the treatment of women became one of the chief concerns of social and religious reformers, nationalist leaders, institution builders, planners, policy makers, and social workers. Given the immensity of the problems of women, much more should have been done than was the case. To some of those attempts we now turn.

CRITICS OF CULTURAL PRACTICES

One of the few leaders who not only thought through the problems of women in India, against the background of her history and culture, but also made a superhuman effort to bring them within the mainstream of the Indian nationalist movement – and subsequently into a lobby- and pressure-responding democratic politics – was Mahatma Gandhi. His work in that respect was preceded by the leaders of social and religious reform movements. Raja Rammohun Roy agitated against the practice of sutee, Ishwar Chandra Vidyasagar advocated widow remarriage, Swami Dayananda Saraswati and Ranade strongly supported the demand for educating women, and Maharishi Karve founded educational institutions for women.[6] Education of women and girls was strongly supported by most of these reformers as a means to their wider social emancipation.[7] And so far as the educated girls were concerned, they continued to demand the traditional security along with modern education.[8]

At a personal level, as is narrated in his autobiography, Gandhi was deeply remorseful, and even ashamed, of his own treatment of his wife, Kasturba Gandhi. His self-criticism of such a behaviour led him to a systematic examination of the status of women in India as defined by the semi-religious and judicial texts and as reinforced by social customs and the attitudes of men. As a social reformer and fighter against injustice to disadvantaged groups, including women, Gandhi boldly maintained, as we shall see, that texts and customs which either justified or rationalised injustice to women neither commanded his respect nor compliance.

Within the unequal traditional society of India, Gandhi saw women as a colossal disadvantaged group which cut across caste, class and regional divisions. For him women *per se* were victims of various religious text, which influenced and shaped individual and group behaviour. So too were social institutions and customs which embodied the norms and prescriptions provided by such texts.

For Gandhi, however, women were a special group of disadvantaged people who required a multidimensional approach toward the resolution of their problems. The mere raising of their literacy level and the provision of legal and economic rights would no doubt go a long way but, nevertheless, they would not furnish the necessary and sufficient condition for the resolution of their many-sided problems. Their problems he thought, required a far more comprehensive approach and had so far not been attempted. Consequently, for nearly three decades, from 1918 to 1947, he attacked those problems in a variety of ways.

He was very clear on the question of family and insisted that in their fight against injustice women ought not to destroy that institution which was basic to their very being. At the same time, however, the need to preserve family ought not to be allowed to become an excuse for continuing their status of inequality and subjection. In expressing his views on these and related matters, Gandhi showed a depth of understanding of women's problems which was very rare indeed.

One of the effective ways of dealing with the problems of women, especially in the Indian situation, Gandhi thought, was to talk about it openly and thereby involve both men and women in their resolution. Consequently, right from 1918, when his first article appeared under the title of "Regeneration of Women",[9] to the very end of his life, he openly discussed the problem of women in journals such as *Young India*, which he edited. As a rule for his journal he had adopted a different style. He would invite questions and comments on the problems of women and then extensively comment on them. That was then followed by discussion on the same problems in various public meetings of that period. Gandhi thus reached a large segment of the public and interested them in questions relating to the need to improve women's conditions.

In those meetings, Gandhi repeatedly went back to the cultural source of the problem, namely, the holy texts and, in particular, *Manu Smruti* or the *shastras* which sought to justify the inferiority and subject status of women *vis-à-vis* men. Such sentiments were embodied in what subsequently came to be known as the Hindu Law. To Gandhi passages in *Manu Smruti* such as "she gains a high place in heaven by serving the husband" (Manu 5–145) and "there is no higher world for the woman than that of the husband" (Vasishtha 21–14), were "repugnant to the moral sense", and therefore something must be done to challenge them.[10]

He also blamed the judicial administration for having formally endorsed many of the customs and practices emphasised by the Hindu Law. What it should have done instead, he maintained, was to apply ancient prescriptions implicit in it, and only after reformulating them in the light of common sense and natural justice. Consequently, Gandhi began emphasising the need for changes in the law governing family, marriage and property.

Before Gandhi the various social and religious reform movement leaders had also expressed their dissatisfaction with the system of law, but could do precious little to change it. So far as the western-educated liberal-minded Indians were concerned, most of them on their own had given much greater measure of freedom and equality to their women than the social customs and laws prescribed. The problem was for the mass of women. Gandhi, therefore decided to involve them in agitational politics so that through it one day they might be able to attend to the problems of inequality which deeply concerned them. At the same time, along with the agitational route, he also wanted women to set examples of courage and self-reliance, which would then persuade men to change their attitude to women in general in a fundamental sense.

Then there was the national movement which was Gandhi's full-time preoccupation. For him such a movement was more than a fight against the alien rule. It was, from his point of view, a movement, simultaneously for the individual's and society's regeneration after their prolonged period of fossilisation. Such a movement, therefore, offered to everyone, and in particular to the disadvantaged groups including that of women, an opportunity to overcome, at the individual and group level, their deeply ingrained sense of inferiority, inadequacy and inability. Consequently, for him, the triple purpose, i.e. individual, social and political, had fused together in the national movement.

He also believed that women's participation in such a movement would not only vitally change the nature of the movement itself, but also alter the nature of the emergent society and women's role in it. Gandhi's view in that sense ran parallel to that of Karl Marx, when the latter maintained that when human beings mix their labour with nature or any social situation, they not only change them but also change their own being. Gandhi, "the fighter saint", did not want women to let go of such an historic opportunity which would help them to break out of their traditional social confines.

From a strict political, and logistic, point of view, Gandhi needed a large number of steadfast *satyagrahic* (non-violent) fighters for his mass movement against the alien rule. He also believed that police and army violence against unarmed women, for reasons of shame, would be much less as compared to that against men. But even if there was equal punishment for the *satyagrahic* women, they rather than men, had much greater capacity to endure physical pain. This is because women, as it is, go through life with much greater physical hardship and grind than do men. For Gandhi, therefore, they, the women, made much better *satyagrahic* soldiers.

Gandhi also believed that such a political experience, of fighting and enduring hardships for what they believed in, would transform the psychology of all those women who participated in the struggle and, through the example set by them, all those women who deeply identified themselves with such fighters. As long as the national movement against the alien rule was on, their energy would be devoted to the overriding goal of Indian independence. But after that, as political fighters for what they believed in, they would be able to organise themselves and fight their own battles to help build a new social organisation which would then offer them justice and equality. Like the prolonged Indian national movement, the quest and struggle of women for what is rightfully theirs, Gandhi knew, would be a long and almost interminable struggle.

Gandhi also believed that Indian society had never fully recognised the extraordinary moral and physical strength of women, which shielded them whenever they underwent suffering for something they believed in. In that respect they had repeatedly proved themselves to be stronger than men. In his words, "To call women the weaker sex is a libel; it is man's injustice to women. If by strength is meant brute strength then indeed woman is less brute than man. If by strength is meant moral power, then woman is immeasurably man's superior."[11]

Apart from their capacity to endure, both physically and morally, much greater grind, women have been, through the entire social evolution, at the centre of the human family. It is around them that various cultures and civilisations have developed. Unfortunately, they were assigned roles which were not always in keeping with the size of their contribution. Nevertheless, up to this point, barring a small minority, they have cheerfully endured their secondary position rather than demand equality of status.

Ironically, their sacrifices and willingness to settle for the secondary position have also given them an added moral weight in certain cultures, and in particular the Indian. Their role as mothers was always revered, though not that as wives or daughters. Indian culture, as Radhakrishanan maintained, held in high esteem suffering for others. And in the minds of men that quality of women was far more established when they, the latter, played the role of self-abnegating mothers.

But Gandhi did not want them to settle for such partial recognition. He, on the other hand, wanted them to come out with a superhuman effort to fight for justice and the recognition

of the true worth of their roles. And, traditionally speaking, the
surest way to go about it was by means of examples of self-
ennobling and self-elevating sacrifices.

Throughout her history, India has been an elite-led and elite-
influenced society. Even the *Bhagwad Gita* stated that the average
man or woman derived the rules of his or her right living from
the demonstrated behaviour of the extraordinary individual
among them. Gandhi, on his part, wanted to use this deeply
ingrained tradition in Indian culture to be able to persuade
women leaders, and other potential women leaders around them,
to set stunning examples of the fight for justice for women so
that others may derive inspiration from them. Repeatedly in his
writings and public speeches, he cited the examples of Damay-
anti, Draupadi, Sita, etc., who set extraordinary examples, by
their sheer moral courage and capacity for sacrifice, for what
they believed in as women and wanted recognition for from men.

At the same time Gandhi the pragmatist also knew that such
extraordinary women, setting examples for others, were very rare
in history. And that along with great vision and demonstrated
examples of individual greatness one also needed adequate
enough social and legal institutions which embodied the rights
of women. He, therefore, came out with the following position: "I
am uncompromising in the matter of woman's rights. In my
opinion she should labour under no legal disability not suffered
by men".[12]

The recognition of equality between men and women, in legal
and institutional terms, led Gandhi to raise the question of its
realisation in actual male–female relationships. For this purpose
he started off with a basic assumption: "Man and woman are
equal in status, but are not identical. They are a peerless pair
being complementary to one another; each helps the other, so
that without the one the existence of the other cannot be
conceived; and therefore it follows as a necessary corollary from
these facts that anything that will impair the status of either of
them will involve the equal ruin of both."[13]

Gandhi was horrified at the thought that to be able to get
their claim to equality recognised by men, women should be
prepared to do all kinds of work which men do or have to do.
Consequently, he wanted to delink the problem of their equality
from the sameness of work and relink it with the kind of work
which was essential to their beings *as* men and women. Least of

all he felt that women should not accept the definition of what work is which is solely deduced from what men do. What women do, as work, apart from what both of them do, should also be recognised as work. To accept the categories, limits, and definitions of work, which are solely based on what men do, would inevitably take away the status and recognition from work which women do as women. Similarly, to agree to do work which only men can do, so as not to be left out of the drive towards equality with men, would merely do harm to women's essential nature. Gandhi, as could be expected, was shocked at the idea that women, in the name of equality, be asked to move around with guns. He did not want guns for anyone, least of all for women. Women, he believed, in their post-subjection period, should not be asked to do everything that men did. To accept that as the test of work would be tantamount to letting men decide what is or is not work.

For Gandhi it was necessary to recognise the equality of work done by men and women on farms and in offices and factories. Equally necessary was the recognition of the importance of work of each in areas of special interest or function. In that respect, women's contribution to the rearing of children, and to the maintenance of family, for which they needed a block of time or phase in their life, also needed to be recognised as work which was unique to their being. Consequently, Gandhi saw no contradiction in women doing outdoor work at certain stages of their lives.

The cycle of work through which a modern woman goes – of initial full-time work, then part-time work or no work outside while she is bringing up her family, and then a return to part-time or full-time work – was very much in keeping with Gandhi's thinking.

What would not have been acceptable to him, however, was the evaluation of women's work for the family as work of not much consequence. Equally unacceptable to him would have been the contemporary emphasis of woman to be paid, by husband or society, directly to bring up the family. He saw her work for the family as her special privilege and a labour of love on her part.

Gandhi thus viewed the problems of women from a different point of view than did Marx. To Marx the main source of the problems of women was that in a bourgeois society they had become some kind of a belonging or property of men. Since women did not do much outdoor work in such a society, they had become dependent on men. Consequently, the only way they could gain their independence from men, and with such an assertion of their own equality, was by becoming "productive units" of society, contributing directly to production in a material sense of the term.

To Gandhi, however, the economic liberation of women was only a part of the answer to women's problems. For him women were not merely different kinds of "men", capable of producing material wealth and thereby claiming their equality with men. For him there was much more to women than being merely the coproducers of material wealth. Their function of rearing children and bringing up a family was as much a part of work, in a broad social and human sense of the term. He believed that the bourgeois degradation of women could not obviate the importance of the family to human beings as such. Political activists and ardent feminists, within the broad rubric of women's studies, are now beginning to rediscover the soundness of such a position.

At the root of their differences there was the different kind of importance attached to different functions *as* work. While Marx did not minimise the importance of women's work in bringing up a family, he also saw the supreme importance of economic work as the criterion imposed by the very nature of bourgeois society. Marx was thus arguing his case at the height of the results of three hundred years of laissez-faire industrial capitalism, what it had done to women and what was their escape route from it in order to regain their independence.

Gandhi, on the other hand, was looking at the problems of women in a traditional society with its interrupted and uneven development which had given to its women the most unfair and inhuman treatment. Such a treatment had its own sanctions in the traditional culture. His first line of attack was, therefore, against those norms which gave their support to women's inhuman treatment. At the same time, however, he wanted a new definition of what work was, so as not merely to let men dictate what it should consist of. In doing that he felt that women would be able to earn the recognition for what they do as indoor–outdoor workers in their much wider range of activity.

Gandhi's legacy of struggle for a better deal for the women of India was quickly forgotten after his death. Only in the last decade was it revived by social workers and feminists, and also by advisors to planners. Since Gandhi worked for the protection and advancement of all the disadvantaged groups including the untouchables, tribals, religious minorities, and women, it was difficult to single him out as one who fought for women.

So far as women's problems were concerned, Gandhi had greater success in involving individual women, and women leaders working for women's causes in the main stream of pre- and post-independence politics. However, his onslaught on those religious and juridical texts, which had condemned women to a position of inferiority, achieved precious little. For women to begin achieving some measure of equality and justice much more than criticism of social practices and holy texts was needed. They needed legal rights and institutional provisions. But more than that, as we shall see in this work, what they needed was the constant mobilisation and building up of their individual and group political capacity to be able to utilise all those rights and provisions.

INSTITUTIONAL APPROACH

The task of building the legal and political institutions of India, within which her citizens could realise the ideals of freedom and equality, fell on Nehru. And Nehru, the institution builder, also showed an extraordinary understanding of the peculiar problems of women in India. He was fully aware of the subject status to which the religious and judicial texts had condemned women, and how the rigidity of the British judicial administration had interpreted those texts in the dispensation of justice. Together with that he was also aware of the part women in India had played, side by side with their menfolk, in the struggle for freedom. He was, therefore, deeply sympathetic to their aspiration for equality of status. Right from the early days of Indian independence, as we shall see, he was keen on making institutional and public policy provisions for the realisation of their aspirations. But in so doing he did not always get the cooperation of his colleagues. Consequently, a number of his proposals had to be either fragmented or modified so as to avoid conflict and confrontation with his orthodox colleagues.

Nehru was aware of the fact that the main brunt of the

prolonged social destabilisation of India, lasting for nearly eight hundred years, from the eleventh to the nineteenth century, was borne by her women. In addition to that, despite being one of the most humanistic civilisations, Indian social organisation had given a raw deal to a lot of segments within it, including the women.

On his part, therefore Nehru very much welcomed the efforts of social and religious reformers, and of Mahatma Gandhi, to involve them in agitational politics. While the elite women had started organising their own groups in towns, from the nineteenth century onwards, what surprised Nehru most was the massive number in which they, as well as the women of lower classes, had started joining Gandhi's Civil Disobedience Movement. In his words, "Women had always been there of course, but now there was an avalanche of them, which took not only the British government but their own menfolk by surprise."[14]

Further, "Here were these women, women of the upper or middle classes, leading sheltered lives in their homes – peasant women, working-class women, rich women – pouring out in their tens of thousands in defiance of government order and police *lathi* (truncheons). It was not only that display of courage and daring, what was even more surprising was the organisational power they showed."[15]

Like Gandhi, Nehru also wanted women to join the national movement *as* individuals and not as women, and thereby start off on an equal footing with men in one of the most important struggles in Indian history. "In a national war," said Nehru, "there is no question of either sex or community".[16]

At the same time he, like Gandhi, believed that such participation by women would trigger off a social revolution in India which would then help them find a rightful and just place in family and society. In Nehru's words, "The call for freedom had always a double meaning for them (women)". It not only meant freedom from alien rule but also a possible and realistic freedom from what he called "domestic slavery".[17]

While Gandhi had hoped that the politicisation of women through the national movement would help them to learn to solve their own problems, Nehru looked to their problems in specific economic and legal-institutional terms. Nehru's own socialist background had persuaded him to look at the problem of freedom *qua* freedom as a consequence, by and large, of economic freedom. Viewed from such a perspective, women in the past failed to get their fair share, either from men or from society, because they, the women, were economically dependent. Consequently, he maintained, "Freedom depends on economic conditions even more than political ones, and if woman is not economically free, and self-governing, she will have to depend on husband or someone else, and dependents are never free."[18]

Nehru, however, neither returned to this theme of the economic base of freedom, later in his political career, nor did he, as Prime Minister of free India, directly address himself to the economic disabilities of women. Most of his efforts were directed, so far as women were concerned, to removing their legal and institutional disabilities.

In 1950, he placed before the Indian Parliament what was known as the Hindu Code Bill. It was aimed at removing some of the inequalities of women within Hindu society. The Bill met with strong opposition from the orthodox members of his own party. As a sheer political strategy, Nehru was then required to withdraw the Bill, chop it up into different pieces, and reintroduce specific aspects of it in different forms. Such a strategy worked. In 1955, the Hindu Marriages and Divorce Act, the Hindu Adoption and Maintenance Act, and the Hindu Women's Right of Succession to Property Act were passed by the Indian Lok Sabha. And, in 1961, it also passed the Dowry Restraint Act.

While the various Acts effectively touched the positions of Hindu women, those of other women, especially in religious minority communities, were left untouched. The disabilities of women in those communities, and in particular the Muslim community, were, in certain respects, greater than those in the Hindu community. But Nehru, and after him his successors, and, in particular, Rajiv Gandhi, refrained from introducing them, and a uniform civil code applicable to everyone, for reasons of minority sensitivity and the possible decline of electoral support.

The institutional and legal provisions made during Nehru's years, did open up the necessary scope for women to attain a fair measure of justice and equality. Nevertheless, women needed to build their own individual and group political capacity to be able to translate such provisions into living realities. Such a potential development of women, as we shall see later on, needed a massive mobilisation which never fully materialised.

ECONOMIC APPROACH

A number of scholars had expressed their dissatisfaction with approaches which merely criticised the traditional values which supported gender inequality and/or made legal provisions for women's rights. Instead they wanted a change in "the established definitions of women's role and status."[19] They also felt that such a fundamental change would come only as a consequence of a change in economic relationships. The three principal exponents of this view are Ivan Illich and Ester Boserup in the west, and Vina Mazumdar in India.

Illich, in his fascinating work *Gender*, made a distinction between gender and sex. Gender, according to him, refers to complementarity, and sex to polarisation, between human beings. Over the years the human condition changed in an unprecedented manner when a transition took place from gender to sex. It gave rise to an "economic apartheid and subordination of women". Such a degradation of women was made possible by the very nature of economic development in modern societies.

And now so very entrenched are the disadvantages of women that our ordinary vocabulary, conceptual tools, and even moral sensitivity, all of them with sexist bias, have difficulty in determining the exact nature of gender imbalance that has occurred.[20]

Boserup, in her highly influential work *Women's Role in Economic Development*, argued that economic and social development lead to the disintegration of existing division of labour in rural communities, migrations to towns, and the emergence of new economic relationships between men and women which are not always to the advantage of the latter.[21]

Vina Mazumdar pointed out that even within the problems of women, those of the upper and middle class received maximum attention. By way of illustration she maintained that the social and religious reform leaders confined their efforts to evil social practices which were prevalent among the upper classes. The demand for the enfranchisement of women in India, after the First World War, was also a demand of those classes. The demand for votes, in particular, vainly created a hope that through such a provision women would be able to set right their fundamental problems of inequality.[22]

Mazumdar thus saw the problem of women as basically a

problem of their economic dependence. In that connection she quoted a passage from the Indian Council of Social Science Research Advisory Committee Report, *Critical Issues on the Status of Women*, published in 1977: "Unless the economic and social utility of women is enhanced in the eyes of their family and nation by opportunities to take part in socially and economically productive roles, the national neglect of women will continue."[23]

In emphasising the inadequacy of political participation through votes, without the socially productive economic activity outside the home for women, Mazumdar's argument ran pretty close to that of Marx. Marx had warned trade union leaders of the latter half of the nineteenth century in western Europe, not to fall prey to the lure of parliamentary democracy. For workers, he maintained, such a democracy, which was rooted in an unequal economic relationship, was powerless to bring about basic social change.

Mazumdar also felt that an historic opportunity was missed in the early days of Indian independence when a number of problems plaguing women could have been dealt with. This is because at that particular time women had emerged as equal *satyagrahic* figurers for independence. Not only that, the highly influential Mahatma Gandhi himself had underlined the need for the removal of economic disabilities of women. What was more, Nehru too had made a herculean effort, in the early years of Indian independence, to remove the various social disabilities of women by means of ambitious legislation. Somewhere down the road the mobilisation of women began to falter and the momentum was lost.

The neglect of the mobilisation of women – whereby they could be made aware, organised, and get involved in a demand-response process of the democratic system and a socially sensitive public policy – was a part of the general neglect of the mobilisation of the people of India after independence. A part of the explanation for this must lie in the post-independence euphoria and an illusory belief in the effortless and automatic progress of a free people. Such a belief was further reinforced by Nehru's enormous dynamism in building the public institutions of free India with a deep conviction that as a free people the Indians will be able to make the necessary social and economic changes by means of the newly introduced public bodies run on democratic lines.

What was, however, lost on a generation of scholars, the political elite, men and women in public life, and the professions in general was the enormous significance of the controversies between Gandhi and Nehru, on the one hand, and Nehru and Jayaprakash Narayan (JP), on the other. These controversies had centred round the question of law of how to keep the momentum of mobilisation, generated by the national movement, going in the post-independence period.

Gandhi on his part wanted to continue the work of mobilising people, on the same scale and intensity, as was done during the pre-independence period. For that purpose he wanted all the topflight leaders to stay out of governmental positions and continue to work in the villages and towns of India as before. He had a deep suspicion of people in public authority even when they were democratically elected. He felt that people in public authority are almost always out of touch with social reality and much more inclined to pursue narrow interests.

Nehru, however, took the opposite view. He believed that as a free people the Indians should be able to make use of the enormous resources of the public institutions for their own development.

Finally, JP, taking his cue from Gandhi's insistence that topflight political leaders should stay out of the business of government, came out with a pointed criticism of Nehru's excessive faith in public institutions to solve the problems of India. From the point of view of JP, India's problems were so very many, and so complex, that paid government servants, no matter how very sincere and hardworking, would not be able to solve them. Moreover, the very nature of their problem had quite a lot to do with their having been a subject people for far too long. Consequently, to be able to come out of it, in a substantive sense of the term, they had to involve themselves *as* a free people rather than be served or be directed by mercenary bureaucrats. Consequently, he criticised Nehru's approach as having an excessive dependence on government institutions, and that instead of such a governmentalism what India needed was the mobilisation and actual involvement of people in solving their own problems.[24]

Although JP's ideas were primarily directed towards those disadvantaged social and economic groups in rural and urban India, who without mobilisation could not effectively use their newly-established democratic public bodies and their decision-making processes, they were equally relevant to the traditionally disadvantaged half of Indian society, namely, women.

Apart from the strength and weakness in the positions of these three giants of Indian society, one thing was clear, and that was that the mere removal of the legal disabilities, and the making of institutional provisions for possible social change were, by themselves, not enough. Such provisions were merely the starting point of any attempt, and a concerted effort had to be launched to mobilise women to learn to benefit from those provisions.

Nearly a quarter of a century of possible effort towards the mobilisation of women was lost in *discovering and rediscovering*, again and again, the wretchedness to which Indian society had condemned them. Quite often, whenever disadvantages of women were identified or reidentified in certain areas, new government institutions were created or new public policy was formulated to set right those problems. Rarely were attempts made to find out the effectiveness of those institutions and policies. And, so far as the problem of the continuing mobilisation of women was concerned, it always occupied a secondary or tertiary position.

At the root of them all women were merely being prepared to become recipients rather than demanders, takers and users, of those provisions so as to change, fundamentally, their position in society and, in that process, their own self-perception. Their prolonged subjection, and the internalisation of notions of inferiority, was not going to be eradicated by the mere presence of opportunities and provisions in the new social policies. Before that women had to be prepared as users of those opportunities and provisions. But this in itself, given the gross mass of social relationships and traditional attitudes, as we shall see later on, was not a simple undertaking. Nor could it be tackled by means of economic solutions only, although such solutions were basic.

The argument that women will be accorded a status and role which are lower than men's as long as they are excluded from what Marx called "socially productive work" does not make much sense in all societies. Women in poor segments of Indian society, in rural or urban areas, have been the cobreadwinners along with their males in the family. The same is true in middle-class, educated urban families. The fact of their earning ability has no doubt given them added importance and even self-confidence, nevertheless, it has neither given them equal status nor fairness in the economic rewards for the work they do. Marx, in underlining the importance of the economic factor as the sole liberating and equating factor, in isolation of other factors, had exaggerated its effectiveness so far as the problems of women are concerned. In this connection, empirical evidence provided by Leela Gulati's intensive case study of "the poorest of poor" working women in the outskirts of the city of Trivandrum is most telling. Those women, who had supplemented their family income, and in some cases were the "principal earners" as their husbands were unemployed, neither rose in status within the social groups to which they belonged nor did they acquire the preconditions of being equal with their menfolk. As breadwinners they were no doubt important to their families. But that is as far as their relative economic strength had taken them. However, *as* women they were paid less for the work they did, and "started at the lowest rung of (work) hierarchy" with no hope of "vertical mobility".[25]

Distinguished American Anthropologist Marvin Harris wrote in his foreword to Gulati's book: "Women in the affluent west often complain about their economic dependence on their husbands and their confinement to the unpaid and undervalued status of housewife. Hence employment outside the household is widely regarded as the key to sexual equality and personal fulfilment. What tends to get overlooked, however, is that the liberating consequences of employment are entirely relative to the nature, conditions, and remuneration of the job performed. For women in underprivileged classes, as for men in similar circumstances, the job market leads to nothing but drudgery."[26]

Since work done by women neither gets adequate compensation nor adds fully to their status within the male–female equation, the question then is whether should we not re-examine the concept of "work" itself, redefine it, and bring out its socially accepted value. Such an attempt was proposed by Kate Young so as to be able to overcome the "invisibility" of women and help them earn their due recognition.[27]

Krishna Ahooja Patel was more explicit in her emphasis on the need to recognise the worth of women's work in monetary terms. Only its quantification and monetisation, as has been attempted in Switzerland will, according to her, give women's work its due recognition.[28]

The fact remains that women's work in isolation of other

actors, neither brought her fair and equal wages nor the added status that it was supposed to bring.

Just as the status of women does not by itself go up simply because they are cobreadwinners with their husbands, it also does not automatically diminish simply because they are unable, for complex reasons, to play that role. How great, for instance, is the dimunition in importance of a women in her role as a mother or wife while she brings up the family? The importance of mother or wife to a family does not go up or down just because she is earning or not earning. Her economic independence may give her a better start in the event of a family breakdown, but the same independence may not bring her the added importance within the family while it is intact.

In treating women as discrete and potentially economically productive units of society, such as the industrial worker, we tend to overlook the other, and more vital, aspect of her being. In practically all societies women are far more deeply involved in bringing up the family, and therefore relating themselves in a complex fashion to a member of family, than do men.

Their role within the family, as its mainstay, as rearers of children, as wives and mothers, forces them to give up or reduce their economically productive role outside home, and to that extent they do not emerge from their unequal condition or periodically return back to it. The question then is how much is this due to her being more involved in family, and how much of it is forced upon her or complied with because of deeply rooted social practice?

The problems of women thus force us to consider them against the background of a network of social relationships, attitudes, practices, and the manner in which all these constrain and prevent them from enjoying a fair measure of social equality with their menfolk. Unless we consider such constraints within living and operational situations, our prescriptions for the amelioration of their problems will have very little meaning.[29]

CONTEXTUAL APPROACH

Before we go further, we need to identify the social contexts within which we can consider the problems of women. Some of these contexts seem to get much less attention than they deserve.

Moreover, the very corpus of theoretical knowledge which we draw upon to understand those problems brings in their limitations and insensitivities. Such a theoretical approach often tries either to seek the replication of western social experiences elsewhere, or to fit, by means of reductionist exercises, aspects of problems of women in India into previously arrived at theoretical frameworks. The only way out of such a distortion is assiduously to reach out to the "givens" of the historical and cultural contexts within which the problem of women in India can be realistically examined. Depending on one's own theoretical perspectives one can come out with an interpretive understanding of such contexts. In this section we shall identify the relative merits of one such approach.

Plurality and Diversity

When we talk about women and their problems in India, we cannot refer to them as a vast gender group with a common set of problems. What we actually refer to, then, are diversified groups of women resembling and differing from one another in an infinite number of ways and manners of their respective problems.[30] In fact the awesome and intellectually intractable complexity and diversity of Indian social and cultural life reflects itself in the equally baffling variety of problems of her women. Consequently, unless we recognise the reality and "givenness" of a culturally diverse world of Indian women in different social groups, in different regions and with different backgrounds, our research into their problems, and our policy proposals to solve them, will have little meaning.

Like development studies, women's studies too are in an early phase of intellectual exploration. And in both of them many intellectually reputable approaches do not go very far because they tend to treat social reality, within an area or social organisation which they want to understand, as one solid monolithic block. They therefore fail to take into account diversity within it. The fact of diversity requires theoretical tools which are designed to identify them and help us come out with explanations which register the nuances of them. And instead of presuming the universal presence of certain problems of women, what we need to do is to build an incremental picture of their researched common denominator.

While the mind-boggling diversity of any Indian social situation or problem is an oft-repeated cliché among scholars, it is also the first victim when they try to fit their investigative operations into a previously arrived at theory in search of universal validity. In Chapter 4 we shall identify the plurality and diversity of the problems of women in a select number of rural communities in a relatively small area in western India.

Network of Social Ties

Historically speaking, Indian society has not gone through the splitting experience of entrepreneurial industrial capitalism and its accompanying liberal political individualism as was the case in the countries of western Europe and North America. Nor did it have anything corresponding to the Roman Law, which sought to establish the individual's relationship with the state, regardless of family relationships. Finally, India did not have any historical experience, similar to feudalism in western Europe, which reinforced the growing sense of individual rights and obligations *vis-à-vis* the authority immediately above oneself. The process of individuation in the west, as implicit in both the Roman Law and feudalism, was fully crystallised by the powerful stimulus of entrepreneurial industrial capitalism, and economic greed, between the seventeenth and nineteenth century.[31] Such forces also refashioned the existing legal and political institutions to permit their own activities, and indirectly, and also by sheer configuration of historical circumstances, gave birth to liberal democracy.[32] What these historical forces weakened were the social ties of ascriptive institutions to which one is born, including the family.

As opposed to that the highly specific individualising experience of India came through religion. It primarily referred to an individual's inner experience and the possibility of infinitely deeper experience, the knowledge and purpose of life, the meaning of human creation, and the supreme design of the maker. Such religious individualism, which dealt with different kinds of issues, weakened neither the foundation nor the social ties within the Indian family. The Indian family system adjusted itself to the extraordinary demands of certain individuals within it wanting to conduct the highly individualised pursuit of inner experience.

Similarly after Indian independence, when India gave herself a liberal democratic constitution, with individual rights and the law courts to protect them, her ascriptive social institutions of family, caste, neighbourhood, religion, village, etc., where associated living and acting are the desirable norms, came to terms with the new demand of permitting individuals to act as individuals while exercising their electoral choices and other rights. Unlike the countries of western Europe and North America, therefore, the introduction of political liberalism did not very much weaken the traditional associated living and acting nor did it introduce a process of fierce individualism. It merely created a commonly agreed jurisdiction for making political choices and exercising certain rights as individuals.

Even the rapid social change of the post-independence period did not very much weaken family ties, although it has changed the character of it in different social groups in different ways. Even the modernised Indians in urban centres, looking at the disorganisation of family life in western countries with their high divorce rate, the plight of single parents, and an uncertain future for children, have begun reaffirming their faith and commitment to family despite all its shortcomings.

In rural and urban India, therefore, it is difficult to talk about the problems of women independently of the family, in the creation and maintenance of which they play a central role. It is equally meaningless to trace back all their problems to their being the creators and creatures of family. Even when we analytically separate them from the family, to be able to analyse and understand the nature of their disadvantages, exploitation and secondary status, we introduce an element of unreality and abstraction.

A similar criticism of treating "the working class" independently of their manifold relationships, was expressed by George Lukacs in his *History and Class Consciousness*. Lukacs, a Marxist scholar himself, felt that far too often Marxists come up with an unrealistic, abstracted analysis of the problems of the working class. Instead of treating working men and women as living persons, with the kind of raw deals that they receive in their workplaces, Marxist scholars often talk about them in the language of abstract relations, which are then expressed in terms of wages, hours of work and productivity, with all of these in quantifiable economic terms. Lukacs felt that realistically speaking there is much more to their human condition than what is communicated by those abstractions. In order to get a clear picture of the condition of the working class we have got to go beyond analytically conceived abstract relations. Any solution to the problems of the working class will not be adequate unless it also takes into account the human beings behind those abstract relations.

Lukacs used the term "reification" (abstraction-making, fossilisation, analytical reductionism, etc.) in connection with the working class, and came up with a plea to broaden the Marxist perspective on it so as to be able to get a more realistic view of that class.[33] Similarly by "reifying" women, and by introducing a culturally extraneous notion of women as individuals in an unqualified fashion, with their individual problems irrespective of the multiple relationships which give meaning to their being, we tend to introduce the notion of abstract woman, abstracted from actual social relations and situations.

Devaki Jain, the humanist feminist scholar, has argued that any goal for women's development which is conceived within the broad framework of "imitating men", is bound to be unsatisfactory, and that instead of making women mimic men, we should try to improve their status, power, and authority, and remove all those obstacles which are in the way of their fullest development within actual social situations. In doing so, she argued that we ought not to destroy their separate identity.[34]

What we need in the final analysis is a notion of justice for women who are bound by the web of *actual* social relations, and not merely abstracted individuals with legal and economic rights. While these latter are basic to their independence, there is much more to their problems than is referred to by the broad rubric of such rights.

To be realistic, we shall have to know the nature of their wide range of problems, exploitations, injustices and disadvantages within the network of human and social relationships and not merely bring in the nineteenth-century European perceptions and solutions prescribed for the then industrial worker. Experience has shown that such a formulation of women's problems in the west did not help them very much either.

Composite Worker

The emphasis on an economically productive role for women as a prelude to their "independence", is predicated on an erroneous assumption. What is true, on the contrary, is that in most societies women are involved in economically productive work. In developing countries a large number of women are involved in their agricultural economies. So then it is not their economic involvement which is in question here but the fairness of wages received and the nature of work done by them, together with the wider, and sometimes almost indefinable, range of their activities and responsibilities. What is more the economic contribution of women, by way of work indoors, on the family farm, in small scale family or commercial undertaking, and/or as landless labourer, qualify them amply as cobreadwinners.

But, unlike men, women have been composite workers. The range of their work is much wider. While men's work is often supposed to be outdoor, and directly related to earning, women's work is both indoor and outdoor, and directly or indirectly related to family earning or saving. Consequently, their problem is not that they are not involved in economically productive work. Their problem is that of society's perception of their work, its evaluation of it in terms of fair compensation, and of its appreciation of their contribution in general.

Furthermore, the perception of their work matters much more when it is undertaken indoors. Since the question of wages for them does not arise while they work indoors, or on family farms or in family shops, their dependence on the family is as much as of any other member of the family. And when they work on the farms of others as farm labourers, wages received by them do not make them "independent" of other members of family. They, on the contrary, become coworkers along with their menfolk and continue their struggle for making both ends meet in a joint manner. Thus their economically productive role is addressed much more to their sheer survivability, especially in developing countries where the rural poor do not find employment all the year round, rather than to using it as a means to their independence. Together, and with togetherness, they come through some of the incredible experiences of poverty. And by themselves, as individuals, they are least likely to make it.

Moreover, in a society like the Indian, which did not have the historical and social experience of individualism, an economically productive role is not related to women's independence from the family or the reconstruction of the male–female equation. What it ensures is the possibility of a continued capability to go to work should something happen to the male.

Ethnosocial Development

What has been consistently ignored by most scholarly works on women's studies is the fact that cast within a network of ascriptive social relationships, which are governed by conventional values and attitudes, and ignored or insufficiently provided for by the bulk of legal and economic institutions and policies, women have, by and large, ceased to develop their own social and political capacity to be able to turn around, effectively, a situation with disadvantages stacked up against them. In a number of cases, despite the availability of opportunities, they did not even try. Clearly in their case, therefore, there must have been far more complex reasons for doing so than in the industrial workers of the nineteenth-century western Europe. Given all the unjust treatment and disadvantages heaped on them since the beginning of civilised living, why did they not develop sufficient will and effort to break out of the situation of disadvantage? Why did they not grow in their human and social capacity to be able to bring that about? While in history, gradually or in a zig-zag fashion, men and women, together, have risen in societies against oppressive authorities, why did the women not rise, extensively, against men who have been a party to keeping them in a situation of disadvantage? The answer to such a question must lie in the complex human situation where a disadvantaged group, instead of developing its own human capacity to enjoy equality and fair treatment, *settles in* in an inexplicable manner and derives deep satisfaction as a group of submerged persons accepting cheerfully what, in most cases, the immediate relatives and kin have to offer. Consequently, while talking about women as a disadvantaged group we cannot talk about one that would grab an opportunity immediately to be able to engage in self advancement. Far from it. In their cases there are as many instances of unused opportunities as used ones. Not everyone in that disadvantaged group has sought recourse to stop being so. In their case the provisions in law and public policy to be free and equal have not been repeatedly used as in the case of men. Absence of mobilisation or consciousness-raising effort can give only a part of the answer.

Young newly-married Indian women walk into a network of antecedent and ongoing social relationships which face them with pre-set sequences of inequalities. Firstly, to be born a woman, is, traditionally speaking – and this is constantly articulated by parents – to be born unequal to men. Secondly, while a woman is married to a man, her marital responsibilities extend to the family of her husband as a whole and not just to her husband. Thirdly, as long as her husband's mother and father are alive, they are the first couple in the family, and then comes her husband, followed by husband's unmarried sisters and then, finally, comes her turn. She, in turn, then puts her own daughters-in-law through a similar sequence of inequalities. Such a cycle is then further complicated in joint families.

Given such a complex web of social relationships, and attitudes and norms governing them, it is meaningless, and even naive, to start treating such women, who graduate from several sequences of relational inequalities, as individuals who are willing and able to start resorting to legal provisions for rights and equalities.

Then there is women's biological urge to be the main keeper of the family. Consequently they, more than men, become the family subsumed persons, make sacrifices in playing that role, get less than their fair share, closely identify themselves with the well-being of all the members, and at the end of the day derive deep and inexplicable satisfaction in playing that role.

In recent years there has been a sea change in the attitude of the leading feminist scholars towards the family. They now see a much more positive role for a woman in the family. Betty Friedan's *The Feminine Mystique* (1974), in which she saw family as a constraint on woman, gave way to family as a means "to give and get love" in her subsequent writing, e.g. *The Second Stage* (1981). Similarly Germain Greer's position also changed from the woman's need to refuse marriage, on grounds of subordination, as expressed in her *The Female Eunuch* (1970), to the need to prevent the break-up of family in her *Sex and Destiny* (1984).[35] Finally, Susan Brownmiller, after a lifetime of playing down the importance of family and children to woman, also went back to them on the grounds that they fulfil biological and psychological needs. These scholars have come to the conclusion that family cohesion is too big a price to pay for a confrontationist assertion of equal rights. The idea now is to bridge the agonising polarisation that has resulted as a consequence of earlier attempts at gender parity.

The basic fact is then driven home, and that is that women's inclination to become family subsumed persons, identifying themselves with the highs and lows of members of family, put them in a different category from men. *Vis-à-vis* men, women thus become individuals with an extra share of family responsibilities.

So while legal and social rights at best make certain provisions for them as individuals, very little is done, or can be done, for them as group subsumed persons. For law and social policy can target them only as individuals, not as wives and mothers who, quite often willingly and uncomplainingly and in some cases even joyfully, give up or do not claim what is rightfully theirs.

It is this latter aspect of their being, of playing the role of the builder and maintainer of their families, which has in effect stifled their ethnosocial development. Such an aspect which, arguably, is a source of a lot of their real problems, can neither be sorted out by declaring women as individuals with rights of their own nor by exhorting them to go and do the outdoor work and thereby become economically productive units of society.

Unlike the small group of educated, professional urban women, you cannot even reach out to women, especially in rural areas, as individuals with their own rights. The bulk of them do not know about those rights, and even if some of them come to know about them, they have little or no inclination to utilise them. Their compensation in terms of feeling good about what they think is right and good for their family helps them go through life with minimum grumbling and complaint.

What is therefore needed in their case is a massive mobilisation to gradually chip away at the gross mass of social relationships, attitudes, ignorance, and deeply ingrained habitual behaviour. As we shall see in Chapter 3, the four examples at mobilisation to reach out to women, as family subsumed persons, and to create new roles and opportunities for their self-involvement, sought to serve such a purpose. The question is then whether their own self-involvement in various participatory processes would make the needed difference to them, and thereby develop their social capacity without vitally affecting their role as the principal builders and maintainers of their family. What they do not want in their role as family subsumed persons cannot be imposed on them.

The mobilisers of women in India, therefore, have the most challenging job in front of them. Relatively speaking, the task in front of Mahatma Gandhi, of questioning the holy texts which reinforced gender inequality, and before Nehru, of building new institutions and making provisions for women's rights and equalities, was easier. The task before the mobilisers of women in rural India, to make them involved in various participatory situations and opportunities and thereby influence their existing social relationships and attitudes, is more difficult. For such efforts are aimed at the very growth of women as disadvantaged beings so that they may be able to break out of the framework of constraints which they find themselves in.

The immediate problems of women in India are located in their relationships with their husbands and in-laws on the one hand, and in their utilisation of the economic and political opportunities and participatory facilities in new institutions on the other. The problems in the first category are essentially of the nature of personal re-equations and readjustments with preferably minimum disruption. In such resolutions, judicial rulings come into the picture very rarely indeed. Moreover, legal recourse for women is not always considered to be desirable. With men and women, the latter is often under an inordinate pressure to give in. Few women are lucky to get their problems sorted out by means of accommodation and plain good sense. Traditionally, therefore, they are in a double bind. They are encouraged to subscribe to the ideals of self-sacrifice and self-effacement. Simultaneously, they are discouraged from having legal recourse to their problems.

The problems in the second category deal with their relationship with their employers, economic organisations, and public bodies in general. In Chapters 3 and 4, we shall see several instances of these. In resolving those problems they have to act in concert with other women and often under the leadership of an urban professional or social worker. Such situations also necessitate the growth of their own political capacity and skill to be able to launch their group activity effectively. In certain rare instances individuals among them show leadership qualities and build not only their own individual political capacity but also that of the group they lead. The point to be made here is that, unlike urban educated or professional women who are aware of their rights, and, in some cases, also possess commensurate political skill to influence the opinions of others or build pressure groups to be able to do so, women in rural India almost always start at the other end of prior mobilisation, group political activity, and then the preparation of individual political capacity to be able to exercise influence and demand a response to and satisfaction of their own problems.[36]

In the foregoing pages we analysed various approaches to the study of the problems of women and pointed out the contribution made by them towards the understanding of those problems. Our analysis also emphasised the need to look at their problems against the background of historical and cultural contexts within which they occur. Such an understanding of contexts also tells us that before we generalise about the problems of women we need to know the peculiar historical and cultural forces which give rise to different kinds of problems in different societies, and that our ability to resolve them would very much depend on how realistic is our understanding of the contexts and situations within which they occur.

2 Urban Women: The Two Generations

In this chapter we shall examine in detail the changing views of women in an urban community towards the role and status assigned to them by the traditional social organisation. Such a change in their views, largely centering around the male–female relationship on the one hand, and the female–society relationship on the other, is far more noticeable, as could be expected, among the younger women than in the older. We shall identify changes in such views of urban women of two generations.

Apart from the generational shift, women's views have also been deeply influenced by the norms of the ethnic and religious groups to which they belong, and by their place within the larger social organisation. The views of women on education, marriage, outside work, divorce, property rights, involvement in family decision-making, etc., are thus not only influenced by their generational exposures but also by cultural values, status, and the notions of personal security and advancement implicit in the social practices of various social groups. What we shall do, therefore, is to undertake a generational analysis of the views of ethnic and religious groups in an urban community. After that we shall see how certain generational concerns cut across such an ascriptive divide.

Distinguished sociologist Karl Mannheim has done a lot of thinking on the question of generational analysis as a means of cutting across social and economic divisions of society by taking into account generational exposures and imprints. He believed that generations get marked off from each other during a period of major social destabilisation. They also get marked off from each other, although much less clearly, by the prevailing circumstances during the period of coming of age of different generations.[1]

Such a tool of analysis is of limited value within the Indian situation. This is because while the generational perspective does help us to cut across those ascriptive social divides, it in turn gets further subdivided by the cultural and religious values of different social groups.

An awareness of such a criss-crossing diversity, depite manifold common influences as a result of urban living, modernisation, education, and generational exposures, would act as a reminder that we cannot talk about women in any society, least of all in India, as one solid block with uniform characteristics and problems, and that our theoretical efforts and general arguments will have to take up the challenge of their mind-boggling diversity as the starting point.

In this chapter we shall first of all identify aspects of diversity in women of two generations in an urban community in western India called Anand. Between the years of 1967 and 1978, I was involved as a co-researcher in a longitudinal research project with A. H. Somjee. That project was designed to look at the intricacies of the democratic process,[2] which are not easily understood by means of previously arrived-at theories and models. That project went on for nearly eleven years. During that period I also got the rare opportunity to understand how women viewed certain social and political issues. Later on in the winter of 1985–6, I designed a specific questionnaire to understand the views of the two generations of women on issues which directly affected their relationship with their menfolk. In this chapter I shall draw upon my findings.

The chapter is divided into the following parts: some approaches to the study of urban women; the urban community of Anand and its women's organisations; the two generations of urban women; some general observations on generational perspectives; and women's leadership and new challenges. We shall now examine each of these in some detail.

SOME APPROACHES TO THE STUDY OF URBAN WOMEN

Let us now briefly examine a variety of theoretical approaches used by scholars to identify some of the changes occurring in the attitudes and values of urban women. These scholars have emphasised factors such as urban migration, economic advancement, education, traditional values, etc., either by themselves or in conjunction with other factors, as influencing the attitudes of urban women in India. In this section we shall briefly examine some of the major exponents of those views.

Boserup, in her *Women's Role in Economic Development* (1970), has argued that when men and women migrate to urban centres in search of economic advancement, they in a sense "telescope a technological revolution" which has been in the making for centuries. By their act of migration they join, as it were, such an ongoing process at a particular point in time. By so doing they shorten the time span, skip centuries, and become participants in such a process and its social consequences. One of the consequences of such a movement, from rural to urban centres, is a tremendous "psychic strain" on the migrants themselves.

Moreover, according to her, what is also implicit in such a migration is the reordering of the economic relationship between men and women. For one thing there is an underutilisation of women's labour in towns which in turn makes them more dependent, economically speaking, on men. Then there are problems of adaptation to an urban environment, which women find more difficult than men.[3]

Further, according to Boserup, the migrant families are suddenly ushered into an economy which is qualitatively different from the one they were used to. In that sense they are pushed "from subsistence production for a family's own needs to specialised production for a market" in a urban economy.[4] That too has its own consequences.

Finally, the range of work which women can possibly do in urban communities is much narrower. There is less scope for them in industries, offices and shops, and more as domestic servants. Consequently, in town migrant women are left with more unutilised time so far as outdoor work is concerned. Such an enforced "leisure" has its own consequences.[5]

Boserup has thus built a general picture of what happens to migrant women in developing societies. However, the condition of migrant women would differ considerably with reference to the social stratum to which they belong. Women in both rural and urban communities do not belong to one homogenous social block. There are variations of ethnicity, class, occupation, income and education among them which, as we shall see in this chapter, make a tremendous difference to their attitude in general, before and after migration.

Then there is the highly specific but fascinating study of Oswal community within the former princely state of Mewar done by Rama Mehta. She pointed out how economic necessity led to an emphasis on education and employment among them. Hardly a generation ago, Oswal women led their sheltered lives in the *zananah* (area restricted for women), with a strict observance of purdah. They could lead such a life as long as the former princely state, in whose court their menfolk worked, provided them with maintenance. When that economic source dried up, particularly after Indian independence, the Oswal women were forced to take education, work before and in some cases after marriage, and move about with much less hesitation in mixed male–female situations. The Oswal girls and women, through education and newly-learnt skills, became indistinguishable, within a span of a generation, from the bulk of middle-class women around them. The main driving force behind the radical change in the attitude and lifestyle of those women, as Rama Mehta has convincingly argued, was their economic necessity.[6]

This then brings us to scholars who have underlined the importance of education, and other related factors, which have influenced the attitudes of women in urban communities. Rhoda Goldstein in her study of the city of Bangalore, in south India, emphasised the part played by "adjustment" as well as "manipulation" in the life of educated women which enabled them to play the traditional role of wife on the one hand, and decision-maker and a person of discrete influence on the other. Educated women, according to Goldstein, received an early training in "adjustments". Their parents who favoured their higher education also, in most cases, did not favour their working outside before marriage. In deference to the wishes of their parents, those educated women brought about their own earlier "adjustments" and then waited for their opportunity to start influencing their parents.

Similarly educated women also received their training in adjusting to the wishes of their husbands. While their husbands did not like them to play the role which their education had prepared them for, both inside and outside the house, they patiently waited for their own opportunity and gradually worked their way into positions which enabled them to play the role they wanted to play. In Goldstein's words, "The most artful women (among them) become masterful at manipulation, learning to wait for the proper time, circumstances and issues on which they can express their own viewpoints."[7] By implication the appearance and reality of educated women's position *vis-à-vis* men is therefore very different.

Similarly, educated or uneducated women wait for their mothers-in-law to decline in authority, which often happens as a result of old age or widowhood, and then gradually start sharing more and more decision-making authority with their husbands.

Goldstein's respondents claimed that their education helped them to become a much more adjustable person, waiting for suitable opportunities or in finding alternative solutions to problems which their families faced.

Such a process of "adjustment" on the part of educated women went a step further. They became, from the point of view of the author, the gradual redefiners of traditional values and relationships without always openly revolting against the ongoing traditional set-up.

Then there is Promila Kapur's study of the emergence of the educated urban middle-class women who are destined to play an important part in changing various social and legal institutions and fight for women's rights. For her the very presence of such a group is "an indication of the significant socio-economic and politico-legal change" in Indian society.[8] The emergence of such a group, according to Kapur, is bound to influence the perspectives of women on two of the oldest social institutions of India, namely, marriage and family. These changes, despite their regional diversity and complexity, deserve to be identified and theoretically analysed. With the help of her own research Kapur illustrated the point by stating that women's attitude to marriage, in particular, had changed, presumably in the 1960s and 1970s, from a "social duty towards the family and community", and a "sacrament solemnised primarily for the fulfilment of one's religious and social duties, and for the welfare of the family", to "marriage as not the only aim" but as a means to having a "husband, home, and children" together with "'material comforts', 'good health', 'individual official status'", etc.[9]

Such were the views of her respondents who were educated women. While the respondents indicated a change in their views on marriage, such a change, nevertheless, did not characterise marriage as a contract. The sacramental aspect of marriage, which is deeply rooted in Indian culture, continued to be the predominant consideration. Like most other social and cultural institutions of India, the relations and obligations within marriage as an institution continued to be couched in religious and moral terms.

Nevertheless, there was a sea change in the attitude of educated women towards divorce, remarriage, and work. A decade before, according to the author, divorce was justifiable on the grounds of "ill-treatment" but, more recently, "incompatability" became good enough grounds for it. Similarly, there was increasingly less and less resistance, on the part of parents, to their daughters' remarriage. Finally, Kapur's educated women respondents also claimed that their going to work, after marriage, did not adversely affect their married life.[10]

But with all these changes taking place in the attitudes of educated women, what must not be forgotten is the fact that women, both educated and uneducated, also played a very vital role in transmitting culture from one generation to another. This point was effectively made by Rama Mehta in her study of western-educated Indian women. She maintained that "Hindu traditions, bound up with domestic rituals and customs, were held together by women."[11] Consequently, they, more than anyone else, provided the basis of family and community life.

What came as a surprise to the author in her survey of the western-educated or the most highly-educated Indian women, was that they too had a deep appreciation of Indian values, saw the need to preserve them, and at the same time subscribed to and pursued some of the modern values which their exposure to the west had imprinted on them.

Thus among the western-educated women, education itself did not bring a distaste for indigenous values. The author concluded that "there was a general agreement . . . that traditional qualities associated with Indian women had intrinsic value."[12] The western-educated women were, in other words, not totally unhinged from their traditional values. They were no doubt more questioning and more disapproving of certain aspects and emphases of those values, nevertheless, they were also confident of bringing about an adjustment between the two sets of values or at any rate refinement in what they found to be irksome.

Those women did not view their education as a possible means to their independence from their husbands but as an additional source for family advancement. The importance of family, despite their full-blown exposure to the west and the weakening of family ties there, occupied the pre-eminent position in their thinking, even beyond their emphasis on spousal equality.

The approach adopted in this chapter may now be briefly stated as follows. The central fact about the social organisation of India is that it is deeply divided on ethnic and religious lines. Each of these divisions conditions the attitudes and values of individuals in various social groups in a particular fashion. To such influences women are no exception. But while the cultural influences fashion the values of various social groups in different ways, individuals within them are also exposed to certain common influences through education, social interaction, work places, urban living, travel, etc. Such common influences then interact with the values of different groups. The nature of such an interaction is different in different groups, and also in different individuals within them. In the following pages we shall identify some of those values underlying the views in certain groups of urban women.

At the same time, however, some of the ethnic groups, or segments within such groups, stand in an emulative relationship with one another. Such segments, despite their cultural condition-ing marking them apart from others, end up by taking more interest in what their counterparts do in other social groups, and also try and emulate their ways to the extent which is ethnically permissible to them. We shall illustrate this point by taking into account the manner in which the younger generation of Kshatriya women, who constantly look to what the younger generation of Patidar women are doing and then try to emulate it in different degrees as is tolerated by their own group.

In this chapter we shall also make a generational analysis of women below and above thirty years of age. The concept of generation, as stated in the previous chapter, is a unique tool of analysis for cutting across the ethnic and religious divide. Through generational analysis we should be able to judge how much the factors of education, urban living, secular social interaction, common workplace, etc. have been able to cut across ascriptive groups at least on certain issues.

The generational analysis of women in India presents its own peculiar problems. To begin with it indicates different kinds of distances, shifts, disruptions and fusions in different groups. The two generations of respondents within the same group often, unknowingly, slide towards each other's position, echo them without seriously subscribing to them, and in general make their respective positions, apart or together, vague or unclear.

Then across the ethnic divide the mother and daughter relationship has a special character to it. While the daugher is a mother in the making, long before her own actual motherhood, or even sufficient apprenticeship for it, she takes on the mother's role as an alternative. In poor families in particular, where mothers have to go to work, the daughter begins to play such a role much earlier. The daughter thus becomes to the family an alternate mom, a supplementary mom, and a sequential mom. The Hindi expression, "badi bahen" is much less pejorative than the equivalent expression in the west, the "big sis".

In a sense the young women are repeatedly reminded by their mothers that they are themselves mothers in the making. This then shortens, blurs or occasionally eliminates the perception of generational difference. What brings it back into consciousness, re-establishing the generational distance, are the factors of education, urban living, workplace, nature of social interaction, and the emulative reference group identification which often cuts across social barriers.

Such generational distances surge and shrink from one exposure to another. They also change from issue to issue, and individual to individual. And such generational distances, as we shall see in Chapter 4, even become indistinguishable in rural communities.

Then there is the mother-in-law and daughter-in-law generational distance, real or imaginary, which is far more clearly felt and expressed than between the mother and the daughter. This is because of the obvious structural difference to begin with, and is then compounded by a genuine feeling on each side about the nature and value of elderly direction on the part of the mother-in-law as perceived by the daughter-in-law, and the upbringing of the daughter-in-law as perceived by the mother-in-law. Since the bulk of women in the younger generation who were interviewed by me were already married, most of them therefore had the status of daughters-in-law. The generational distance in them therefore was more clearly marked.

Finally there was the routine as well as the traumatic mobilisation of women in Anand where the generational perspectives were examined. The routine mobilisation of women consisted of the work done by 18 women's organisations, some of them more active than others. Some of the leaders of those organisations were highly dedicated women. But through those organisations they reached, by and large, the women of the older generation. Such women, who were mothers-in-law, routinely participated in the activities of those organisations. Their involvement was more of the nature of voluntary work towards sending medical, economic and educational help to the poor in Anand and its surrounding villages. Their involvement did not touch the sensitive issue relating to women and their disadvantaged status.

The other mobilisation, which electrified women of the older as well as the younger generation, though much more the latter, was a traumatic episode in 1985, when an upper caste London returned dentist-in-town, was accused of murdering his wife. The dentist, it was alleged, was not happy with the amount of dowry which his wife had brought in. He wanted more. When the parents of his wife refused to give the additional amount, he was alleged to have killed her hoping that he would then be free to marry again and get some more money by way of a dowry. Such an episode brought all the women's organisations together, and they took a huge procession through the main street, held an emotional meeting, presented a petition to the minister in the provincial capital and saw to it that the whole matter was not swept under the carpet by the police. They even set up a committee to investigate and supply information on similar episodes in the town in the past, and to monitor similar problems of women before it was too late to help them.

Such a traumatic episode no doubt involved women of both generations. It was, however, of much greater significance to the women of the older generation. Some of them had experienced similar threats from their greedy husbands, and, unlike the younger generation, were unable to defy them. The background of such an episode had therefore made the younger women think and talk much more on issues relating to marriage, divorce, dowry, property rights and social policy in general. In the following pages we shall now analyse a variety of their perceptions, responses and anxieties.

THE URBAN COMMUNITY OF ANAND AND ITS WOMEN'S ORGANISATIONS

The urban community where generational perspectives were examined is Anand, in the state of Gujarat, in western India. It is a mid-sized town with a population close to about one hundred thousand. This was despite the establishment of several medium-scale industries, an inordinately large grain trade market, flourishing commerce, proliferating complex of educational institutions, and one of the largest milk cooperatives in the world, namely, the famous AMUL. Anand, nevertheless, retained its rural character for a variety of reasons. For one thing there was a constant migration into it from surrounding rural communities. Those migrants retained their ties with the rural communities of their origin. Then there were industrial and office workers who worked in Anand but preferred to go back to several dormitory villages surrounding Anand. They commuted by means of trains, buses, scooters, mopeds and bicycles.

There was also an additional reason why the commuters preferred to stay in surrounding villages. Depending on one's income and taste, some of those houses in surrounding villages had indoor plumbing, electricity, gas stoves, refrigerators, TVs, VCRs and other modern gadgets. People in some of those villages also had relatives in East Africa, Britain, Canada and the US.

Over the years Anand had become a lively centre of education. Its school system was highly influenced by the idealistic background of a number of life-time volunteer school teachers who worked on a small fixed salary, with facilities for housing, medical aid and the educational expenses of the children. These volunteer teachers set the pace and standard of education in the town. The premier among the institutions which they established was the D. N. High School. A large number of district and state leaders were the alumni of those institutions.

Girls' education did not lag behind in Anand. One of the best-known among them was Sharda High School, which attracted a large number of girls of Indian origin from abroad. Their parents wanted them not to be totally uprooted from an Indian cultural background and therefore such a residential school offered them a unique opportunity of not only picking up the Indian values but also of receiving a modern education.

The people of Anand, and of the surrounding villages, built, despite great political resistance, a thriving university, which was then named after the famous Indian freedom fighter, Sardar Vallabhbhai Patel. In that university from the very beginning girls started competing with boys for admission to several fields such as architecture, computing science, medicine, engineering, etc. In 1985, the university had admitted, on merit, a large number of girls to various professional courses. In B.Pharm 60 per cent of students in that year were girls, and in Electronics their number had come up to 40 per cent.

Simultaneously, the interest of boys in higher education in general, especially from families in rural areas, was declining. The boys who came to the university were the children of middle-class urban servicemen. As opposed to them the boys from the rural areas felt that the university education did not help them very much in their economic advancement.

The number of women working in various professions in Anand in 1985 had steadily increased. In kindergarten schools, 92 per cent of teachers were women, and in primary schools it was 45 per cent. In the same year a number of female lawyers were practising in Anand, and at least ten from Anand were practising in the High Court at Ahmedabad, the state capital.

One of the biggest problems concerning how well the girls from Anand had done was that of keeping track of them wherever they went after marriage. Since the bulk of them could not marry in Anand, they took with them their newly-acquired skills wherever they went. As opposed to that the girls who came into Anand showed a slower rate of educational and professional development.

Then there was a sea change in the composition of the nursing profession. The school of nursing in the newly-started hospital in Karamsad, close to Anand, reported at the time of its capping ceremony in 1983 that girls from different social backgrounds had started joining the nursing profession. Formerly the same profession, because of the rigid traditional standard of pollution, had become the sole preserve of Harijan (ex-untouchable) and Christian girls. But now there were girls from all social groups including the Brahmins and Patidars.

Finally, in recent years the women of Anand had enjoyed much more freedom in visiting cinemas and restaurants either in groups or on their own. They also drove an increasingly greater number of scooters and cars, did their own shopping, visited beauty parlours and enormously stimulated demands for saris, jeans, kurtas and beauty aids. Suddenly visits to beauty parlours had become quite respectable, and even middle-aged women visited them before social events. That in turn stimulated a demand for trained beauticians, providing yet another opening to the enterprising women of Anand. Some of them, it was reported, made more money than the average male doctor in the town.

Let us now briefly examine the various womens' organisations in Anand. Established at different times, with different degrees of dedication and dynamism in their leadership, Anand in 1986 had 18 women's organisations. Their areas of activity ranged from the ethnic locale to the far-flung areas of rural communities in the district. The oldest among them was Hariba Mahila Mandal which came into existence in 1951. It, and several others established after it, largely devoted their attention to the running of schools, mostly *anganwadi* (kindergarten) for the children of the middle class, and circulation libraries for books and magazines. Then came in 1964 the Inner Wheel Club which has remained most active since its inception. Its major undertakings were in the medical, nutritional and educational fields. Over the years it has succeeded in arranging health camps for treating ailments of the eye in various villages by persuading medical practitioners to donate their time, skill, and medical resources in helping the rural poor. It had also sent textbooks and exercise books to needy children in those communities. Moreover, in Anand as well as in adjoining rural communities, they had distributed medicine without charge, helped immunise children against various diseases, and taught mothers how to get most nutritive value from the food that they prepared for their families. Later on they coordinated their health work with the Tribhuvandas Foundation which undertook to launch a health scheme for the whole district. We shall examine the work of the latter, which is entirely rural, in Chapter 3.

Finally in 1985, Jagrut Mahila Sangathan came into existence which sought to bring together all the women's organisations of Anand under one umbrella so as to be able to mobilise women and rouse their consciousness towards injustices done to them. Its foundation and work was made easier by the notorious case of the dentist accused of murdering his wife.

Most of these organisations centred around their founding

leadership, and its ability to involve women with some background of education, whose husbands were sympathetic to
women's causes and issues, and whose children were grown up
enough to look after themselves while their mothers were away
doing periodic voluntary work. In a sense all the women leaders
in those 18 women's organisations depended on their husbands
for moral support and on their experience of similar involvements.
None of those women leaders could function as they did against
the wishes of their husbands. Quite often it was the husbands of
those women leaders who got them involved in their own
voluntary activity first and then persuaded them to start organisations for women to address similar problems of the latter.
Consequently, all the women leaders unfailingly pointed out how
much they owed to their husbands.

Barring instances of wife-battering, wife-burning, desertions,
and continuous extraction of financial consideration from the in-
laws, the bulk of women leaders were not inclined to look at
either the gender relationship or gender treatment critically or
in an overly sensitive fashion. Most of these women leaders did
not even want to question the culture of *purush pradhan* (male
dominance) which is deeply assimilated in the social fabric and
in the actual gender relationships of Indian society. But within
such a structure of relationships, these women also wanted to
build for themselves the role and status of companions, confidants
and spouses that lend dignity to the husbands on social occasions,
both traditional and modern, and prove themselves as "useful"
in the eyes of their husbands first and then the society in general.

These women thus proved their usefulness by going beyond
their traditional role of wife and mother, and as the centre of
the family, to individuals who were deeply involved in their
children's education and their husband's professional advancement, and remained as a back-up force for the entire family no
matter what the problem was. In mid career of husbands,
especially when their children had grown up, these women had
begun to play an extraordinary part in acting as a force in
building up, whenever necessary, not only the morale of their
husbands but also in helping them to find ways and means of
their own development by thinking aloud before their wives and
by benefiting by their involvement. These women leaders had
moved within their own families playing a variety of roles and
discovering their own proliferating usefulness in areas which

they themselves had not visualised before. The leadership of
various women's organisations, and also the bulk of their active
membership, was made of such women. Their own unassuming
ways had helped them to ingratiate themselves to their women
following.

As women they did not address their efforts to attaining
equality with men but in going in search of new roles for
themselves, within the traditional gender relationships, where
personal equations got constantly restructured as new mutualities
and dependencies evolved. Initially such new roles were social,
going out with their husbands or playing the part of active
hostess, accompanying them on their travels, helping them by
taking messages and transmitting directions, instructing people
and taking charge of the education, even the higher education,
of their children. They also got involved in decision-making
process when their husbands wanted to think aloud on various
alternatives and choices to be made. After securing such a
role for themselves, these women went out to build voluntary
organisations or work in the existing ones. But there again their
husbands were either directly or indirectly in touch with the
working of those organisations.

THE TWO GENERATIONS OF URBAN WOMEN

Let us now briefly examine some of the specific attitudes of the
women of the older and younger generations in the town of
Anand. Since such attitudes are conditioned to a great extent
by the social background of those women, we shall first of all
undertake such a generational analysis against the background
of the caste or religion of those women, and then cut across those
divides to be able to make a few general observations on
generational differences among women. As mentioned earlier, in
1985–6 I had ascertained the views of the two generations by
means of a survey to supplement my earlier observations, with
the help of a stratified sample. This sample included women from
social groups such as Brahmins, Banias, Patidars, Kshatriyas,
Christians, Muslims and Harijans. The respondents in the
sample were then grouped together as those below thirty years
of age and those above it. The following is an analysis of those
responses.

Brahmins

The Brahmins, the priestly caste, had put considerable emphasis on education as well as on cultural values. Such concerns were also reflected in their womenfolk across the generational divide. The Brahmins of Anand had a number of sub-groups among them. But the major group among them was known as Bajkhed-awal. They had registered their economic ups and down over the centuries. Their priestly profession had furnished them with a lot of liquid cash which then helped them to act not only as moneylenders but also as the buyers of large tracts of land whenever they became available. Since the beginning of the century they had experienced an economic downturn, losing most of their land to Patidars, and supplementing their loss of income by taking modern education, going into professions and working in offices. Their emphasis on education had also extended to their women. While such an emphasis gained ground among their women, it also lent approval to their going out to work in offices, and in various professions, first of all before marriage and then after it. Work before marriage was considered to be an outgrowth of education, but work after marriage had to wait till women overcame the inferential stigma that their husbands did not earn enough and were therefore forced to put their wives to work.

Both generations of Brahmin women saw a great advantage in the education of women. To the older generation, education furnished protection to women, as it became an "armour of self-defence" against wily individuals in society. It also provided, they believed, a means to economic independence should that become necessary. Education for them was thus a weapon in store. More than that it could also give a better start to their children in a highly competitive world of professions and service.

The younger generation of Brahmin women, most of whom had already obtained high school or university education, had already experienced such competition *as* women, and were neither inclined to scale down their ambition nor settle for the secondary, traditionally assigned, positions for women. They did not show hesitation on the question of going out to work after marriage. Such a question, they thought, should be settled by women themselves. Unlike the older generation they did not want to limit their work opportunities to what was described as the "suitable" professions for women, such as teaching, secretarial work, etc.

There were identifiable differences between the two generations on questions concerning marriage, divorce, involvement in family decision-making, etc. The older generation had welcomed the shortening of marriage ceremonies, the obtaining of the consent of the boy and girl before marriage, and not making the girl's side feel the "inferior" of the two. The younger generation felt that the girls should have more say in the choice of their future husbands. Mere consent to anyone selected by parents was not good enough.

The older generation was inclined to treat marriage as something which concerned more than the two individuals involved. For them it was the coming together of the two families. In the event of the failure of marriage, the prestige of both families was at stake. Therefore, the woman, who has a greater capacity for sacrifice, should "endure" whatever her marriage brings. As opposed to that, the younger generation of Brahmin women, while they did not take divorce lightly, considered it to be the only way out of an unhappy marriage. What they feared most was the future for the divorcee. Where would the divorcee go if the parents or brothers did not offer shelter? Thus, according to them, society too should make it easier for them to get out of an unhappy situation by helping them to find suitable work.

Banias

Another important social group in Anand is that of the Banias, the merchant caste. Like the Brahmins they too had several sub-groups within them. Being a social group engaged in trade and commerce, they had often sought to work with the most powerful economic group in the area, namely, the Patidars.

For the older generation of Bania women, education was more important for the future of the boys than the girls. Education of girls, no doubt, made them better mothers, who in turn could more effectively look after the economic advancement of their male children. As opposed to them their younger generation of women saw education as a means of their own economic advancement first, and then that of the family. Moreover, for them with education a woman could enter the professions or get a job in a bank or government office. Among the male Banias, however, working for others was never the first economic choice. Traditionally, and even hereditarily, they were known for their dislike of working for someone else. There were, then, their educated daughters who, economically speaking, wanted to go the other way. Since there was no such thing among the Banias as female entrepreneurs, except in some rare cases where they had inherited the family business, the only economic use to which their educated women could put their education to was by seeking employment in offices, and, in very few cases, by pursuing professions on their own.

There was much less marked difference within the two generations of Bania women on the question of marriage and divorce. The women of the older generation maintained that since woman finds her home, children, security, status and destiny though marriage, it should be taken very seriously. The younger generation agreed but also added the possibility of the breakdown of marriages. But then they maintained that divorce was relatively higher among the Patidar women than in any other they knew.

Patidars

This then brings us to a numerically large community in Anand, namely, the Patidars. A major part of their lives revolved round the matrimony of their children. Even their economic pursuits, and they were wide ranging, revolved round the problems of finding sufficient money for the dowry of their daughters.

The Patidars of Anand, and in particular of the district of Kaira, where Anand is located, dominated its agriculture for centuries, and, more recently, its commerce and industries. They also dominated its educational, cultural, civic and political institutions.

The Patidars of Kaira are mostly Leva Patidars, as compared to the Kadava and Anjana Patidars of the neighbouring districts. The Leva Patidars are highly respected by the Patidars of other districts for their hard work, doggedness, innovative spirit, economic drive, emphasis on education, and social development in general. The Patidars of different districts do not intermarry. They observe strict endogamy whereby they have their own designated villages to which they give their daughters in marriage, and another set of villages from which they bring brides for their sons. The Patidars also remain obsessed with their internal hierarchy and treat the matrimony of their children as a means of registering a higher status within it.[13]

Since the turn of the century, no other social group had registered a greater social change than did the Patidars. They continually improved their economic base, extending from agriculture to commerce to industry, entered middle-class professions, travelled extensively inside and outside the country, and cultivated a highly innovative and pragmatic outlook. Despite that they allowed a blind spot to develop in matters of the marriage of their children. A part of the answer to this puzzle can be found in the relatively recent reorganisation of the matrimonial circles within the community.

During the Moghul administration, and later on during the British raj, the Patidars earned the confidence of their rulers and entered into their revenue bureaucracies. Some of them adopted surnames such as "Desais" or "Amins" which indicated their past status as revenue collectors. In course of time such families came to have higher status than those of others within the Patidar community.

Later on their hierarchy-making thrust started expressing itself in terms of specific village locations. The first claim to superiority, by means of village location, came with the formation of what is known as the six *mota gams*. They are Sojitra, Karamsad, Nadiad, Dharmaj, Vaso and Bhadaran. They constituted themselves into a separate *gol*, or a matrimonial circle, indicating wherefrom girls can be brought in, and to which villages girls can be given in marriage. Implicit in that *gol* formation was an assertion that they now constituted the Patidar aristocracy. Five other villages, after prolonged negotiations and efforts, were given an auxiliary status of *mota gams*. They were Uttersanda, Ode, Pij, Nar and Sunav. After that the Patidars of other villages desperately started setting up their own *gols*. Those new *gols* were known by the number of original villages in them. Later on more were added but the initial number, as *gol* identification, continued. Thus there came into existence the *moti satyavis* (the big twenty seven with many more villages in it than the original number), *nani satyavis* (the small twenty seven), etc. Each of these stood in an acknowledged hierarchical relationship with the initial *mota gams*, but among themselves their superiority–inferiority claims were always in dispute.

So far as the *mota gams* were concerned, they practised what has been appropriately called an open hypergamy.[14] That is to say that a Patidar from other villages could marry his daughter to a boy in one of the *mota gams* provided he paid a good enough dowry to sweeten the deal. The amount of dowry depended on the status of the girl's village and also on the ability of her father to pay. If such a village was considered to be an undistinguished village then the amount of dowry was correspondingly higher. Most *gols* also maintained a published roster of eligible boys in their circle.

On their part the Patidar fathers wanted to marry their daughters to *mota gam* boys so that their grandchildren may have a *mota gam* as the village of their origin. Such an achievement not only raised the status of their grandchildren and gave them a better start in life but also helped their own *vis-à-vis* their peers.[15]

Even within the other *gols*, the parents of the girls had to pay the dowry. The rate of dowry, locally known as *paythan*, related to how the boy's family and his own economic future was perceived. In recent years, demographers have been talking about the shift which seems to have brought down the proportion of marriageable girls to boys. The social impact of this, however, is yet to be felt on the matrimonial markets of the Patidars.

Such social values and practices directly affected not only the economic condition of the average Patidar family, but also the attitude to the upbringing of their daughters. Patidar parents with boys and girls to marry claimed that the system did not affect them adversely. But parents with more girls than boys, or just girls, grumbled and anguished a lot and hoped that their caste leaders would do something to get rid of the dowry system.

The parents of daughters made known to them, directly or indirectly, that they, the daughters, were a liability. That was then internalised by the daughters as their being burdens to their families. With the spread of education among Patidar girls, such a sense of burden often resulted in an airing of views against the Patidar system of marriage and dowry.

Over a period of two decades, in urban and rural Gujarat, where I was involved in field research, I met a large number of Patidar families. Almost everyone within them had hoped that more education and a general awakening among the Patidars would put an end to the evil practice of dowry. The sad fact is hat it did not. With more education of boys, the rate of dowry also correspondingly goes up. Patidar boys settled in Britain, Canada and the US, ask, and get, more dowry. So very organised is the system of dowry extraction, by parents of boys who are settled abroad, that they announce through the matrimonial columns of the local newspapers by which airline flights their boys would arrive, their immigration status abroad, and in particular their US green card, and when they would be available for an exploratory talk on matrimony. Interviews are usually arranged in posh hotels. Sometimes some of these boys are grouped together for a display and interview and, as an irate educated Patidar girl put it, it is like a cattle market waiting for the highest bidder.

While all that goes on at the level of the parents of Patidar girls, they themselves now take higher education in an ever-increasing number, and have experienced a radical change in their views on education. We shall analyse this against the background of the two generations of Patidar women.

The older generation of Patidar women perceived the education of women as a means to better housekeeping, the maintaining of household accounts, and bringing up a family. They did not view education as an insurance against future difficulty in marriage or widowhood. Nor did they favour the idea of women going out to work, especially after marriage, as this reflected adversely on the status of the family.

The younger generation of Patidar women, however, looked at education and work after marriage from a different perspective. They were inclined to link education with their own economic independence should the need arise in the future. Moreover, they had their own misgivings about the future of their marriage. In that sense they were realistic observers of the social scene around them where a number of Patidar girls were subjected to torture, humiliation, wife-battering and burning, and continuous pressure for abstracting more money from their parents. Plagued by the dowry system, despite phenomenal economic and educational development within the community, the younger Patidar women, with limited means, had learnt to delay their marriage, and sometimes for too long. And even when their parents procured them with husbands, with their own economic resources stretched to the limit, there was no end to the greed of their husbands and their families. While their parents agonised, and often buckled under the renewed pressure, they, the girls, often came to the brink of making drastic decisions to commit suicide. They often toyed with the idea of divorce, more than in most other social groups, and registered a relatively much higher rate of divorce. And although no reliable figures of the rate of suicide among Patidar girls are available, they are considered to be pretty high, and in Gujarat in general, about the highest in the country.

According to Patidar women of the older generation, girls these days ask too many searching questions about boys before they give their consent for marriage. Gone are the days when they could be persuaded to say "yes" just because the parents had made a decision. Some of the girls even wanted to make discreet enquiries about the boys, on their own, before they gave their consent.

More and more Patidar girls have now started bringing their own choice of boys home for their parents to look over and approve. These young women usually meet those boys either at university or at their place of work. The choice of such boys often creates a problem of *gol* or marrying within strictly defined matrimonial circles for the sake of the purity of the blood. In the tussle that follows, in such cases, an ever-increasing number of young women win out. Sometimes they are forced to flout the wishes of the parents, incur their displeasure at the beginning of their marriage, and then patch up later on.

The younger Patidar women were fully aware of the change in their own views on marriage and the extent of acceptance of such a change by their elders. One of my young respondents put this as follows: In the days gone by it used to be said of the daughters and cows that they would go wherever you lead them. Now they both go their own way. This sentiment was expressed in Gujarati as follows: *dikari ne gai, dore tnya jaya*. That has now changed to, *dikari ne gai, fave tnya jaya*.

Those respondents also said that parents can no longer be sure of the automatic acceptance of their own choices by their daughters. In fact a lot of small groups, though not enough, consisting of young men and women, have sprung up in several of the towns and villages of Kaira, to oversee and bring to public notice the excesses of dowry. Parents of girls are ambivalent towards it. No doubt they want a discussion on dowry before marriage which should be honoured by boys' side. But once a deal is struck, they resent any interference from these matrimonial vigilantes. So far as parents of boys are concerned, they are downright angry at this new development.

There was also a marked difference in the two generations of Patidar women on their involvement in the family decision-making process. The older generation of women were forced to accept whatever their husbands did not want to discuss with them. With such an attitude also came humiliating remarks such as "not your cup of tea", "does not concern women", "women have much less brains, even the *shatras* say so", etc.

The younger generation of Patidar women did not accept their exclusion without making a fuss. For one thing, most of them were educated, sometimes as educated as their husbands. They were often quick to retort that the same *shastras* also made them the *grahalaxmi*, the goddess of family well being, which therefore required their extensive involvement in family decision making.

Such a stand, taken by the younger generation of Patidar women, did not by itself change the gender equation at home. But implicit in that stand was a position which could not always be ignored by their husbands. In the overlapping decision-making areas the younger women had made continual gains. Such gains ironically enough also relieved their husbands of the anxiety of having to make those decisions all by themselves.

The Patidar social scene was thus full of extreme contradictions and shifts. Within it there were instances of widespread ruthless dowry extraction, existing side by side with the spread of boys and girls making their own matrimonial decisions. One could quote as many cases of wife harassment as those of a liberal attitude and a high degree of involvement of women in the decision-making process at home and in matters relating to their husband's place of work. On the side of the parents there were a large number of cases where the parents literally bought US-resident husbands for their daughters only to find out that they were no good. Such an experience and repentence continued side by side with the cattleshow-like parade of the would-be husbands in the posh hotels of metropolitan cities. The Patidars thus had not sorted out the problems of one of their basic social institutions, namely, marriage. It roused strong emotions and at times divided the community on generational lines.

Kshatriyas

This then brings us to another numerically strong group o
inhabitants of Anand, namely, the Kshatriyas. The Kshatriya
were not one single cohesive group. Within them there wer
differences of ethnic purity, of place of origin, and of matrimonia
circles. At the top of their social hierarchy there were the pur
Rajputs, who traced their ancestry from the various rulin
families in the area. Then there were those who worked a
warrior chiefs in the courts of various princes. Finally the bull
of Kshatriyas were considered to be a cross between Rajpu
soldiers and local Koli women who were considered to be of low
social status.

The Kshatriyas of various hierarchical levels had very littl
social interaction among themselves. Each segment within then
also had its own *gol*. Periodically attempts were made t
"homogenise" them by electioneering politicians, but they di
not go far enough.

Economically speaking, the bulk of the Kshatriyas were at th
bottom of society. They were either marginal farmers, semi
skilled workers, odd job workers or landless labourers. Thei
educational level, and particularly that of their women, wa
deplorably low. Despite living in an urban community lik
Anand, their womenfolk had a limited exposure to its modernising
influences.

The older generation of Kshatriya women looked at th
education of women as a means of doing domestic accounting
writing letters to relatives, and putting one's signature rathe
than thumb impression, in short, all the routine functions o
literacy rather than as a means to their economic independenc
and advancement.

The views of the younger generation of Kshatriya women wer
no different. Despite relatively more schooling, they too looke
at education not as an instrument of self-advancement an
independence but something with the help of which you becom
a more efficient housewife. Among them there were a few schoo
teachers and office workers but they had yet to become rol
models for the rest of the women of the younger generation.

The Kshatriya women of the younger generation had not go
round to questioning the unsatisfactory aspect of their gende
relationship as was the case with Patidar women. The older a

well as younger women among them showed deep respect for marriage and family, nevertheless, the younger generation of Kshatriya women pointed out a few disadvantages that their marriage had brought them. Both groups held the view that with their marriage was intimately connected the prestige of the family of their parents. Consequently, they should not do anything to harm their good name. While the older generation wanted everything to be endured within marriage, the younger one had some reservations. The latter accepted the fact that sometimes divorce may be the only way out of a failed marriage. They also believed that their own community had come a long way in that respect and that unlike the old days it was willing to listen to the woman's side of the story in a troubled marriage.

As opposed to the older generation of Kshatriya women, who endured their own exclusion from the family decision-making process, the younger women wanted to have a greater share in it. They therefore constantly probed and tried to know more about the decisions that were going to be taken by their husbands, sometimes risking their self-respect and domestic peace.

Unlike the women of the three social groups discussed so far, the Kshatriya women of both generations who went out to work in fields, the market place, offices, schools, industries, homes, etc., were acutely aware of the fact that they did not get either a fair deal from their employers or due credit from their husbands for contributing to the family income. The older generation of Kshatriya women, as could be expected, were given to silent endurance of whatever their husbands had heaped on them. As opposed to that the younger generation of women were given to complaining about the widespread drunkenness, gambling, wife-battering, and laziness on the part of their husbands. They also maintained that tears in the eyes of Kshatriya women, these days, was a normal sight. But then what was the way out? No woman wants to be a burden to parents or brothers; they have their own problems. And as far as divorce is concerned, nobody has paid any attention to what will happen to a Kshatriya divorcee. So many times younger Kshatriya women, who could not take the mental as well as physical torture any more, thought of walking out on their husbands, but then what was the alternative for them? Some of the younger Kshatriya women mentioned with envy that Patidar younger women often managed to leave their husbands and start a new life for themselves. This

they, the Patidar girls, could do because they had more education
and sometimes even professional training. By way of an illustration the Kshatriya girls mentioned the recent development in
the nursing profession, especially with reference to Patidar girls.
There was a sea change there. The profession was no longer
confined to girls from Christian and Harijan communities, and
Patidar girls had started joining it in large numbers.[16] Moreover
their parents also helped them out during a period of family crisis.
While the Kshatriya women did not have those resources they very
much hoped that their younger sisters would be able to find an
easier escape from their troubled marriages.

Christians

The Christians of Anand were, relatively speaking, a small
group. They consisted of Roman Catholics, Presbyterians and
Mukti Foj (Salvation Army). Although the Catholics were the
first to start their proselytising work, and to build several
institutions, the Salvation Army, because of its educational,
social, and medical work, remained the most active group within
them.

Like the Kshatriya older women, the older Christian women
too considered the education of women as a means to better
living and housekeeping. As opposed to that the younger
generation of Christian women, who had come through various
Christian educational institutions, were keenly aware of the
usefulness of education to them in a highly competitive and
prejudiced society. They also believed that for their economic
and social advancement as a group, education was indispensable.

As stated earlier, the nursing profession in Anand, which was
a preserve of Christian and Harijan girls in the past, had seen a
tremendous change. Girls from all castes had started entering it
with much more education than was available to the Christians
in the past. This new competition in the field was treated by
them as a signal for tougher days to come when they would have
to work hard and train better to be able to retain their advantage.

The younger generation of Christian women, given the precari-
ousness of their traditional occupation of nursing, treated education as a means of their collective survival as a group rather
than as a means to restructuring the gender equation within it.
Threats to their cultural identity as a group, as well as the need

survive in competition for jobs, had reinforced the bonds not
only of the group but within the families as well. As individuals
and as families they had acquired a deep commitment to their
group. Only its survival could guarantee their survival. The
group consideration thus made the women of both the generations
look to marriage and family very protectively. Since husbands
and wives were jointly involved in group efforts, the idea of
divorce and independence from a husband remained very much
in the background. The routine stresses and strains in their
family life were sorted out by the involvement and help of near
and distant relatives, leaders of the community, well-wishers,
and religious leaders.

Muslims

The Muslims of Anand too were a diverse group. Apart from
the usual groups of Sheikhs, Sayyeds, Moghuls and Pathans
among them, there was also a well-knit group of Vohras, who
were shopkeepers and semi-skilled workers.

Both generations of Muslim women favoured the education of
women. The younger generation, in particular, felt that the
education of Muslim women would help them to look after the
education of their children more effectively.

The older generation did not want women to go out to work
after marriage. As opposed to that the younger women felt that
since these days it was quite respectable, and secure, for women
to go out to work, married Muslim women should not shrink
from it. They felt that it would help not only in family income
but also to broaden the minds of women. They also felt that
the younger generation of Muslim women should take more
education and come out of their sheltered existence.

The Muslim women of both generations welcomed the new
provision for divorce for Hindu women. Since they already had
such a facility, they could understand the reasons for it. They
were, however, not keen on discussing the extraordinary privilege
enjoyed by Muslim males in divorcing their wives. While a
national controversy was raging over the issue of Muslim personal
law in 1985–6, questioning the continued advisability of having
any separate personal law based on religion, the Muslim women
did not want to share their thoughts and anxieties. They in fact

did not want any outside interest or interference in their persona
laws.

Harijans

This then brings us to the Harijans, and among them the Venkars
The Venkars, whose traditional profession was weaving, usec
to make use of animal gut for their work. The contact with anc
the use of such a material dragged them down to the traditiona
classification of untouchables. This they have deeply resentec
for centuries. Over the years, in order to get away from such a
condemned status, the Venkars of Gujarat had worked extraordinarily hard either as agriculturists or semi-skilled workers or
landless labourers. They had also put an enormous emphasis or
education, and migration to urban centres, in the hope that their
children, through such efforts, would be able to escape the
ignominy of their traditional status.

Such single-minded ambition also extended to their women
They too had hoped that the education of their daughters was
bound to lead to an improvement in the educational attainments
of later generations. Consequently, the educational institutions
of the villages and towns of Gujarat are full of Venkar children
whose educational achievements are way above their traditiona
social status.

The older as well as younger generation of Venkar women
expressed great eagerness for work at all stages of their lives
From their point of view they did not find enough employment
because of their low social status. They therefore eagerly
demanded greater opportunity for work so that they could
supplement their family income.

Since the Venkars were at the bottom of the social and
economic ladder, theirs was a joint undertaking, with women
working side by side with men to work their way up. Consequently, the involvement of women in family decision making
was almost equal. Their poverty, reinforced by their low social
status, from which they were trying desperately hard to escape
had brought men and women not only much closer to each other
but had also put them on a near equal footing. In almost every
respect they seem to be the co-equals of each other. Among them
one did not hear the norm of *purush pradhan* (male superiority)
or the gender disparity as one did among the Brahmins, Banias

and Patidars. The Venkar low status, which had cruelly taken away their human dignity from them, had, ironically enough, bestowed upon them, in many ways, the near gender equality. Still lower down, among the tribal women, as we shall see in Chapter 4, the scales of relative importance were turning more and more in favour of women *vis-à-vis* men as one of the givens of their social and economic life.

SOME GENERAL OBSERVATIONS ON GENERATIONAL PERSPECTIVES

Let us now make a few general observations on the generational perspectives of women in the various ethnic groups that we have analysed in this chapter.

It is abundantly clear that women of both generations were deeply conditioned by the positions and norms of their social groups within the hierarchically-ordered social organisation on the one hand, and by the extent of their exposure to the new forces and values of a constantly-changing urban society on the other. Such positions and norms were far more clearly identifiable among the various social groups than within the generational groups with their common exposures. Then again, depending on specific issues, the generational issues were more easily identifiable in the higher social groups than in the lower, or in the religious minorities.

Moreover, the exposure to the new values of an urban society, particularly on the part of the younger generation of women in the upper social groups, does not totally wipe out their traditional and ongoing set of values. The new values, on the other hand, compete for acceptance and, if accepted, interact with those which are already there. And those which do not coalesce with what is already there then become a focus of a new aspiration or vision, awaiting wider acceptance.

Then there are instances, as in the case of the younger generation of Kshatriya women, of those who fell within an emulative group, wanting to emulate the younger women in higher social groups, and thereby got their exposure to new influences second-hand.

There are also the extreme cases of generational cohesion among those social groups which felt that their cultural identity

was threatened or which put together a group effort for their
economic advancement. In each case they acted as a group
blurring the generational distinctions within them. This was
particularly true of the Christian, Harijan and to a lesser extent
Muslim women of two generations. Such an enforced cohesion
as we shall see, did not bring to the surface their latent gender
stresses. In their cases the over-riding considerations were so
pronounced that they made their internal differences unidentifi
able.

Similarities and differences in generational perspectives on
education and work after marriage came out clearly across
certain ethnic groups. There was a near identity of views on the
education of women among the older generation of Brahmin
Bania and Patidar women. They all believed that through
education women would be able to improve their quality of
housekeeping and care of children in general, including the
education of the latter.

Those women were also inclined to relate work for women
especially after marriage, to their family status. Their sensitivity
to outdoor work was further heightened when it came to their
daughters-in-law rather than daughters going out to work. For
them the work done by the former, outside the house, was
indicative of the financial standing of the family. Even if they
were forced to work for financial reasons then they should confine
themselves to certain feminised jobs such as teaching, office and
bank work, etc. Such gender-specific work was acceptable to
them for their daughters and, as a second choice, for their
daughters-in-law. If, however, their daughter-in-law happened
to be a professional person, i.e. doctor, lawyer, professor, etc.,
then the sensitivity to their going out to work was much less.

The older generation of women in those three groups also
exercised enormous influence on the nature and extent of change
in the thinking of the women of the younger generation. While
the older generation of women were gradually changing their
own outlook on things, they were also a factor, both as mothers
and mothers-in-law, in making the necessary difference to the
newly-acquired values, and operational freedoms, of the women
of the younger generation.

Despite the criticisms of and open disagreements with mothers,
on various issues concerning marriage, family, work, women's
rights and responsibilities, the daughters fashioned and devel-

ped their own perspectives and attitudes within the framework
of norms laid down by the mothers. They no doubt nibbled away
at that framework and changed it as they went along.

The influence of the older generation of women on the
daughters-in-law was however greater. Unlike the daughters
who enjoyed greater freedom and tolerance, usually shown by
parents, the daughters-in-law had to follow strictly the lines laid
down by their mothers-in-law. And even when they acquired
their own relative ascendancy over the mothers-in-law, due to
the old age, infirmity, or widowhood of the latter, they rarely
radically departed from the lines already laid down.

Consequently, the generational differences, in terms of the
values, perspectives and attitudes of the women in those socially
higher communities, which had outwardly appeared to be much
wider were, in fact, operationally and realistically much less so.
The structural relationships between the two generations in the
final analysis brought them much closer to each other, and both
sides gave in a little. The younger generation either phased out
its demands so as to adjust itself to the pace of change the older
one was capable of, or reduced them as it graduated from the
status of daughters to daughters-in-law. The threat of disruption
or fear of split between the generations was much more verbalised
than was actually the case. As the pace of social change in the
urban community picked up, so did the time span needed to
adjust. While generations adjusted themselves their talk about
what it was like "then" and "now" continued. In that context
the Gujarati and Hindi terms, *jamano*, and *zamana* respectively,
indicating changing times, were most helpful in expressing one's
feelings and were judiciously used.

The differences between the two generations of Kshatriya
women were not on work after marriage but on the condition of
women after marriage and the recourse left open to them. In
that respect they were far apart. Their differences were, in the
final analysis, on how much the women should be asked to endure.
While the older generation counselled limitless endurance, as
there was very little to choose between a husband's or a mother-
in-law's ill-treatment, and the community's gossip and criticism,
the younger generation verbalised the possibility of trying out
different things after marriage. They saw the changing character
of society as viewing the plights of women in failed marriages
more sympathetically. For such Kshatriya women of the younger

generation, Patidar women in a similar predicament. Walking out of the husband's household or divorcing him, and then standing on her own feet, was the model to imitate. While the parents of a Patidar woman in trouble were willing to stand by her, the Kshatriya woman was not very sure of the same treatment. Consequently, without subscribing to the endurance philosophy of their older generation, the younger Kshatriya women, with all the psychological preparation to do something about their unhappy situation, could not walk out of their failed marriages. They neither had enough education nor moral courage, nor precedents, to make it on their own.

Unlike the upper social groups of the Brahmins, Banias and Patidars, where differences between the two generations of women were smoothed out by mutual accommodation and influence and also unlike the two generations of Kshatriya women where their philosophical positions, despite inaction, remained different, the positions of the older and younger women among the Christians, Harijans and Muslims, to some extent was one of rallying round the family and community to be able to protect their cultural identity, seek economic advancement, and also gain higher social status, all of these by means of group effort. Such considerations, therefore, narrowed and dampened down the generational differences between them.

WOMEN'S LEADERSHIP AND NEW CHALLENGES

Let us now briefly examine the views of some women leaders who, over a period of two decades, tried to mobilise the women of Anand and rouse their consciousness on several issues facing them. So far as the bulk of women leaders were concerned, there were very few new faces among them over a period of nearly twenty years. Some of them had become less active than before and those who remained active throughout had registered changes in the way in which they looked at women's problems and the solutions to them.

There was another significant point which needs to be mentioned here about the developing countries. A political leadership which attains power after its involvement in a national movement, and also gets involved in building and operating new institutions, often tends to stay on in power too long. Sometimes its duration in office extends to a period when, in normal circumstances, the succeeding generation should have had an opportunity to get into power. Consequently, such a leadership can be described as a two-generational leadership. Some such thing was also noticeable in the women's leadership of Anand. What we shall do, therefore, is to record the significant changes in the perception of issues, and the nature of the involvement of the same leadership over a period of two decades in office.

In 1973 and 1974, I interviewed a number of women educators and voluntary workers. Most of them were involved in the women's movement in Anand. Then in 1985–6 those of them who were still around, together with a few more, were interviewed again.

In the 1970s, the women educators believed that women would learn more from each other rather than by means of prescription or advice. Within that women were more inclined to learn from those who had themselves suffered for what they believed in. The mythological tales of the heroism and self-sacrifice of Indian women, and also the suffering of those who were involved in the Indian national movement, and were brutally beaten up and jailed, were the most effective examples for others. So then what was most important was an example of demonstrated conduct. No one moved women more effectively than such individuals.

The women educators also believed that women leaders had a very difficult constituency to nourish. While there was so much to be done to help women, they, the women themselves, were the least willing to look for such help and the least able to help themselves. This is because most of them were too overwhelmed by family responsibilities to be able to do anything else. Such a predicament, therefore, puts an enormous burden on the women's leadership into their efforts to carve out and serve a clientele which is so much wrapped up in its own world.

A decade later, the approach of the same and other women leaders was different. Gone were the days when they used to talk about personal experiences. Their emphasis now was much more on organisation and work in specific resolvable areas within their larger problems. They had, in other words, acquired a much more pragmatic approach to those problems.

Women's organisations in urban and rural areas were now training women in new skills which could help them make readily marketable goods. These consisted of handprinting, embroidery, weaving, quilting, etc., with traditional and new designs. Then there was the manufacture of bags, sheets, tableclothes and pillow cases with designs supplied by designers with a good eye on the market. Top business houses marketing such goods were asked to help out in determining what would sell, and then their help was enlisted in marketing them. Then there was the involvement of women in rural areas in co-operative dairying, which we shall examine in detail in Chapter 4. Such involvement had helped women economically and socially. More and more women's organisations were coming up in rural areas which were getting involved in consumer's issues. Finally, there was the phenomenal growth of the education of women, which as we examined earlier, had made them more informed members of women's organisations.

On the whole, according to those educators, the shift in the picture could be summed up as follows. Formerly parents of unmarried girls told them that marriage, husband, family, and the prestige of the family was everything for a woman. While such advice still continues, the younger women on their own, looking at the changing times, have also started taking their own education, work, participation in domestic decision-making, and watching and learning from more educated and professionally-established women, more seriously.

The other two segments of the women's leadership in Anand consisted of women political party workers and women voluntary workers. Over the years, there was a considerable turnover in the former but very little in the latter.

The political workers of the 1970s did not look at the women of Anand as a special constituency for them to nurture, or as individuals with special problems of their own. Their problems were considered to be those which affected the whole family, for example, the rising cost of living, and the disappearance of articles such as sugar, edible oil, medicines, etc., from the open market. Therefore the way to help women was to ensure regular supplies of groceries and other articles. Those political workers also saw women as totally dependent on men, and their contact with them was, therefore, only through their menfolk. In return the men were requested to tell their women about the vote or some other kind of support which the women political workers needed. Direct access, of women to women, therefore did not develop.

Fittingly enough, the women political workers were themselves men-appointed women leaders, and they in turn were inclined to view women as having no identity of their own. They therefore had very little to do with women or their problems. Nor did they make any effort, with the help of their common sense or intuition, to discover what women's special problems could be. Since they had already made it in a man's world, it was good enough to take things as they came.

However, the major problems of dowry, desertion, wife-battering, and female backwardness in general did receive their attention. But they also had the usual do-nothing solution for them and that is that with education and development all those problems would automatically disappear.

In the decade of the 1980s, when the women of Anand began to make their presence felt, both as people with special problems and as voters, the women political workers gave them the access to administrators and ministers. Without doing much for the women, these politicians, as could be expected, climbed on the bandwagon whenever an issue giving them good publicity was around.

The case of the women voluntary workers of the 1970s was different. Since politically they were free from the need to enter into the influence structure built and sustained by men, they displayed a far greater understanding of the problems of women. They gave occasional expression to them, but after that they too withdrew from positions which would involve them in agitational strategies which would embarrass middle-class families. The decade of the 1970s waited, as it were, for these voluntary women workers to grow up and then effectively zero in on their social work efforts which involved, over and above the routine social work and agitational work, the lobbying of ministers and administrators, and the taking of certain cases to lawyers. Such an added role did not come easily for them. They felt far more comfortable in arranging the administration of free medical camps, providing facilities for triple vaccine for children, giving subsidised milk to infants, collecting discarded eye glasses and recycling them for further use with the help of opticians, holding special eye camps, and giving part-time work to women rolling papadams and making pickles, etc. What finally brought them out of their routine social work were the increasing instances of wife-battering, the "suicides" of young women who saw no way

out of their hopeless marriage, and the consequent realisation
that they were not addressing their efforts to some of the most
burning problems of women.

Although the individuals in positions of leadership had not
changed significantly in the 1980s in Anand, they, nevertheless,
were required to respond to different kinds of problems. Among
their followers now there were a large number of women with a
university education, experience of professional work, including
medical and legal work, increased national and international
travel, and with frank views and ideas which had begun to
change the very nature of gender relationship on the one hand,
and the relationship between women and society on the other.
Such a following had gradually placed before the leadership a
new agenda. The women's leadership, consisting entirely of
voluntary workers, was quick to recognise it and was persuaded
to take action on it.

Moreover, this was precisely the generation of leadership
which was deeply influenced by the perceptive writings of the
well-known Gujarati feminist writer Kundanika Kapadia, and
especially her widely-read book *Saat Pagala Akashma*, which
underlined the need for feminine realism and frankness in gender
relationships.

Without giving up its ongoing work, which was so vital, the
leadership took on more responsibilities. Since some of the
women came from a medical background, or were wives or
mothers of practising physicians, their medical work among
women and children had already earned wide acclaim. Then
there was the work done by them in the fields of nutrition,
hygiene and education. To those concerns they now added the
problems of dowry, especially among the Patidars, wife-battering
and desertion among the Kshatriyas, group-submerged women
in the religious minorities, and Harijan women struggling for
the recognition of their basic human dignity, at the lowest level,
hoping that some day their children with education and economic
advancement, and with people with greater humanity around
them, would treat them as equal human beings. Thus the newly
sensitised women's leadership discovered the special problems
of women in general but also the specific problems within various
groups.

Ironically enough the problem of dowry among the Patidars,
which then acted as a catalyst for the identification of other

problems of women, was highlighted in those families which had
education, experience of travel, and a professional background.
The Patidar families which had emigrated from East Africa, and
from there to Britain, were considered to be the worst dowry
givers and takers. The British Patidars, in particular, on their
matrimonial visits to this area, while deriding the "backwardness" of the local Patidars, engaged in material transactions
relating to matrimony which made the marriages of their boys
and girls of secondary importance.

Consequently there was increased concern over what was
actually going on in western India's community of high achievers.
In almost every other respect the Patidars had distinguished
themselves. This included education, agriculture, commerce,
industry, the professions, politics, social work, economic advancement abroad, etc. Why, then, did they not take care of what was
happening to their institution of marriage and the future of their
daughters? In the mid 1980s, the thinking was that the problems
of their women would not be solved by other background efforts;
that they will have to face it frontally. The Patidars had produced
a large number of social workers, both men and women, in their
ranks to take up the issue. The case of the alleged murder of a
local dentist's wife convinced them of the urgency of it.

The women leaders also began to realise that their work was
far more onerous and complex than they had previously thought
or had experienced. Besides the sympathetic and enlightened
men with whom they had always worked, they would now be
required to work with the police, lawyers and administrators,
not to mention men accused of the ill-treatment of their women.
They began to realise that so far their role had been reactive,
one of catching up with tragic events which had already taken
place. The question now was whether they could prepare their
followers to spread word around for advance or timely help. Not
only that, their new monitorial responsibilities might bring them
into head-on collision with some of the well-established, educated
professional families who might also ask them to keep their noses
out of other people's business.

Within their following itself, the women's leadership for the
first time had a group of educated, gender conscious radicals on
its hands. It consisted of a small unorganised group of young
women with a university and professional background. They
wanted more than what their traditional and unchanging position

had condemned them to. Their education, coupled with an imported style of gender conflict and confrontation, had made them, individually, very articulate. Their anger, however, had not crystallised into a critical agitational group which could then act as a spur to the established leadership. Most of them, as a matter of fact, had not even met any like-minded individuals. Apart from the changes in their own points of view and values, they were full of veneration for the established leadership. Consequently, what they wanted, without expunging the traditional values, was the infusion of new ones which would then directly influence the restructuring of gender relationships.

For the established leadership, which had extended its lead to the following generation, the new arrivals did not constitute a threat in a culture where age and experience were still venerated. To begin with, they were just like new faces around with more education and greater self-confidence. In the past such new faces had always come in waves, made noises, and then settled down. So would these. Moreover, one could easily ride them out by merely showing sympathy and doing what one wanted to do in the first place. Since no one wanted to be thrown into an uncharted sea of limitless change, everyone clung onto and appreciated whatever little acceleration in the pace of social change was beginning to take place. So while the leadership was in a position to quieten down the radicals, the radicals for their part, were also in a position to hasten the pace of change, in a limited way, in the area of gender relationships.

All in all the women's leadership in Anand was coming of age by discovering that apart from routine social work it also had the responsibility of paying attention to the gender relationships within the various segments of society which, as we saw earlier, presented a diverse and complex picture. Most of those relationships, reinforced by the attitudes of men and society, and by traditional values, had condemned women to situations of disadvantage. And for them to cut through the maze of those attitudes, values and practices was indeed a formidable undertaking. In the following chapter we shall see how a piecemeal approach to them, whereby you slice up the gross mass of problems into manageable specific units, bore effective results.

3 Urban Elites and the Regenerative Processes

Women leaders in India are deeply aware of the fact that women in rural India are greatly in need of their mobilisation effort and of practicable suggestions to help improve not only their economic condition but their social status as well. Since more than two-thirds of the population of India lives in her villages, with limited exposure to the forces of modernisation and facilities for education, the task of the urban women elite is that much more difficult. Most of the urban-based women leaders are aware of those difficulties. But their problem is where and how to begin. The immensity of the problems of rural women, and their mind-boggling complexity, have discouraged many women leaders from even trying their hand at them. They have often rationalised the fact that they are too few and that their time is all spent looking after the problems of urban women.

In this chapter we shall describe and analyse the nature of the effort of several urban women who did try to mobilise rural women, and in one case rural migrants to city, despite a lot of obstacles, and earned some measure of success in their effort. Through their efforts they tried to broaden the scope of work which women could do and thereby helped them attain a better status for themselves and even enhanced security. Through their efforts also the urban women leaders helped at the chipping away, as it were, at the gross mass of traditional relationships and attitudes which had put women in those rural communities in a disadvantageous position. Simultaneously, through programmes of instruction, training and supervision, they helped those women to learn to involve themselves in various social and economic processes and thereby attain some measure of self-development through self-involvement.

In all those instances, as we shall presently see, the various urban leaders had some measure of success because they addressed their efforts to the highly specific problems of women. They meticulously sliced away those problems, as it were, and addressed their efforts, in specific areas, in a highly practical and problem-solving manner.

This chapter is divided into the following parts: seeking a deeper involvement in cooperative dairying; new functions in health and hygiene; new attitude to women at work; demanding union and public policy protection; and some general observations. We shall now examine each of these in some detail.

SEEKING A DEEPER INVOLVEMENT IN COOPERATIVE DAIRYING

Within the last four decades milk cooperative dairying in western India, and in particular in Gujarat, has come a long way. In the various districts of Gujarat it has established a cooperative milk grid, phenomenally increased the output of milk and milk products, provided an extraordinary quality of animal healthcare, improved the quality of milch animals by means of programmes of balanced feed, artificial insemination and cross-breeding of animals, substantially increased the supplementary income of milk producers, and achieved all these goals within a democratic set-up at both the village and district level.

The spread of dairy cooperatives in the rural communities had also vastly increased the scope for women's participation in it. Despite being the principal managers of the milk economy – which involved feeding, scrubbing and bathing the animal; looking after its health generally and keeping an eye on the critical periods for artificial insemination; finally, milking it and taking the milk twice a day to the village milk cooperative regularly – women had left the participation in decision-making bodies to their men. Such a division had often created an artificial atmosphere in those decision-making bodies. Quite often those men sitting on various committees did not have a clear idea of what the actual problems of dairying were. At the other extreme women who had quite a lot of first-hand experience of dairying, did not have direct access to those bodies. In order to overcome such barriers in the way of women, and also work towards the possibility of increased milk productivity, the extension department of Amul dairy, India's premier milk cooperative organisation, in cooperation with the Kaira District Cooperative Union, decided to appoint a number of trained women instructors to go from village to village in the district, to address women and make them aware of the constant changes in the techniques of feeding, milking and breeding that were taking place in the field of veterinary science, and also exhort them to get involved, actively, in the various decision-making bodies and thereby develop new interests and roles for themselves. They repeatedly reminded the women that the milk cooperatives belonged to its members and to no one else. Most of the instructors had a university degree, were outgoing, and as they went along, they had cultivated the knack of reaching out to the tradition-bound women and involving them in a suggestion–implementation relationship on the one hand, and in public discussions relating to their problems of dairying, on the other. In this section we shall examine the nature of such an effort and its consequences.

The veterinary personnel of Amul nostalgically recalled their experiences in various villages of the district three decades ago when the milk cooperatives were being established in the remote villages of the district. The information about the animal communicated to them during those days used to be second-hand, abbreviated and often distorted. This was because while the woman of the house had looked after the animal, she could only communicate its health problems to the vets through an intermediary, i.e. the husband. The husband in his impatient, fumbling and ineffective manner would then communicate those problems to the vets. That then led to yet another phase when the partially emboldened woman would either correct or supplement the version of her husband from inside the house, usually from behind the half-closed door. Then there was the recent phase, in this evolutionary process of shortening the distance between the vet and the woman, when she would stand either by the door, with her *laaj* (end of sari duly drawn over a part of the face) and indirectly, as it were, answer the questions the vet asked about the animal.

Such a gradually attained boldness, on the part of the woman, also helped her overcome the constraints placed on her contacts with outsiders in general. Such a development also facilitated the movements of the vets and stockmen. They could now freely move from door to door and talk to the woman of the house, who was invariably there, rather than wait for the man of the house to turn up from the fields.

The dissolution of the woman, man and vet triangle in animal upkeep also helped the vet to start building an effective two-way channel of communication between the woman and himself for trying out new ideas. While the vets had most of the theoretical and bookish ideas, they could learn a lot from the actual implementation and reportage by the woman. But in most cases the problem of male–female distance between them still remained. Despite the establishment of such a communication link, the ability of women to act effectively on what the vets wanted them to do was only partly utilised. The women needed someone they could relate to at their own level.

This need of a follow-up, and also of a second line of communication from woman to woman, was filled by the specially trained women instructors. As opposed to vets and their assistants who remained obsessed with productivity, animal health and breeding, and thereby spent the minimum amount of time in the village, the female instructors could talk to women in the broader terms of family and children as well as dairying. Moreover, women related better to one another and had much less feeling of embarrassment while discussing awkward issues relating to animal reproductivity.

But sooner or later, women instructors had to move on to other villages. There were only six of them in 1985–6 trying to cover the entire district of nearly one thousand villages. Consequently, the instructors were forced to plan their own obsolescence in every village they went to, and got deeply attached to, and its women to them. Their job was to prepare those women animal keepers to be more receptive to what the vets had to say. On their part the village women wanted their human bonds, newly forged, to go a little further in time. While it was not possible for those women instructors to stay on longer than what their own tightly-drawn programme required, revisits by them to their favourite villages and families within them were full of excitement.

At the end of their visit the female instructors did make the rural women more receptive to the vets. The vets had now become for the women the "bosses" of the instructors, busy doctors rather than embarrassment-causing male strangers. The instructors themselves constantly reminded women to put all their problems before the vets rather than remain quiet out of sheer shyness or embarrassment. Such exhortations often worked wonders. Others emulated what the emboldened women among them were able to do. In the course of time the vets and their assistants became for the women of the village a part of the dairy infrastructure often referred to as the "dairywallas". The more the instructors tried to link women to vets for all their dairying problems, the more they reduced their own functions as intermediaries. Socially speaking such a linkage was likely to revolutionise the world of the rural women. For the first time they were being brought in regular contact with men from outside the family, kinship or village structure. Such a linkage was forced upon them by economic necessity. For them it was the initial step in creating a new social space for themselves from which they could move both upwards and sideways in facing males. There were the shopkeepers, transport people, school teachers, administrative and medical personnel, all males. Since most of them were from outside, a gradually emboldened contact with them was relatively easier. It was as it were a sideways movement for them after their baptism in male encounters with the vet and his male staff.

What was more difficult for them, however, was a freer expression in the presence of their village males, especially the male elders among them, who collectively became for them the elders-in-law. Traditionally speaking, women were required to lower their *laaj* in the presence of them and even refrain from speaking directly to them. Such a social practice was the single most powerful reason for women not wanting to be in the same room or in the same corner of the room and then express their views in public meetings. In such mixed situations only daughters of the village, who enjoy a special freedom of talking to men, or elderly widows, could be without inhibitions. The rest of the women had to practise different degrees of reticence, prodding each other to speak, with indirect and muffled murmurings.

What the female instructors did, apart from their individual contact with women at their own residence, was to gather women collectively, without their males present, and talk to them about their possible involvement in public bodies, especially in the milk cooperative society of the village. And if per chance a village elderly male walked into the room, then like the instinctively obeyed command of an army drill sergeant, the collective *laaj* of the women present went down with a quick flourish.

At such meetings, without males from the village being present (outside males were not much of a problem), the instructors initiated women into asking questions, making comments and giving suggestions, in short in preparing them for a possible public role at a later stage.

The instructor's narration at such meetings acquired a folksy family style of speaking, where the last two or three words in each sentence, which could be easily anticipated, were left to the audience to fill in with a loud collective chant. Such an involvement kept the attention of women riveted to what was being said. For them it was like talking while listening. Specially composed songs, in traditional *garba* (folk dance) tunes, regarding dairying, were also sung, making the dairying a community undertaking.

Then at crucial moments the instructors would bring in illustrations of what traditional wisdom, in animal upkeep, prescribed and how modern science had improved upon it. Suddenly everyone wanted to know what more should be done. After that whatever was put across to them did not need repetition. The illustration at one occasion was that of how many times a day the animal should be served with drinking water. The traditional wisdom restricted it to three or four times a day. The new technique, however, suggested that with more water the animal was likely to give about half a litre of milk more without losing its fat content. Similarly suggestions about shortening the periods for artificial insemination, new kinds of cattle feed, cross-bred cows, etc., all became common knowledge with women at the end of their individual and collective instruction.

After that came some psychologically more complex questions. One of them was "to whom did the milk cooperative belong?" The women were told again and again that they owned it as its shareholders and it was they who employed and paid wages to the whole lot of people including the secretary, vets, stockmen and the entire body of "dairywallas".[1] Such answers were more easily repeated by them than genuinely believed.[2] But time after time women were told that since they were its real *malik* (owner), they should also begin saying so publicly. As the women of the village got more exposed to the instructors, some of them acquired more confidence in asking questions and making comments in public meetings with their own *laaj* duly drawn in the presence of the male elders.[3] The bulk of them did not get past murmuring a few words amongst themselves. The problem before the instructors was, therefore, how to transform the widespread culture of murmurs in public meetings into a culture of questions, comments, and better still, of participation in the organisation itself.

From the point of the instructors it was relatively easier to make women into better animal keepers than effective participants in public bodies. After nearly a decade of dedicated work, the six women instructors, with their repeated visits to villages, had succeeded in improving the attendance of women in the general body meetings of their respective villages. A number of villages in the district reported that as many as one-third of the people in attendance were women. And some of them had started asking questions. The questions related to grievances over the determination of the fat content in milk supplied, and on which depended the payment of money and the availability of cattlefeed, and rarely over organisational matters such as the shrinking size of the annual bonus and the reasons for it.

The instructors had thus achieved some degree of success in moving women from their total absence, silence and murmurs to presence at meetings and questions. The next stage was to help them to acquire the culture of participation, by overcoming shyness and social constraints, and that by any standard was a herculean task. By mid 1986, the instructors had covered as many as 868 villages in the district, covering a total of 117,276 women milk producers.

What was already achieved was indeed remarkable. In the past the dissatisfaction of women towards the organisation could be expressed only through a male voice. They, the women, had to prod their men to ask those questions. Now women themselves were in the halls of the decision-making bodies, with all the assured legitimacy, authorisation and training, to ask those questions themselves.

Such a shift was beginning to open up for women a new arena for themselves. Since their menfolk were not as deeply involved in the milk economy themselves, they had either a spectatorial or gossipy interest in how the organisation functioned. The concerns of women, however, were different. Their questions and problems were based on their first-hand knowledge and their deeply-felt needs. Consequently, when in future they start participating, effectively, in the decision-making bodies of those organisations, they will bring into them a producer–operator style of efficiency and concern.

NEW FUNCTIONS IN HEALTH AND HYGIENE

Amul, with the help of an army of veterinarians, stockmen and other assistants, was able to set up a highly efficient system of animal health care. Under such a system the veterinarian routinely visited all the villages in the district, went from door to door enquiring about the health of animals, examined them, discussed problems relating to their health care with their owners, gave medical aid and instructions, and kept regular records of the health of animals. On top of that the veterinary staff assured the owner of milch animals, spread over one thousand villages in the district, that it would provide medical assistance to any case of emergency within four hours of receiving a telephone message. Amul was able to do this with the help of its own radio telephone service and roving jeeps, medically equipped, within the shortest possible time.

Such a performance had deeply impressed the villagers. Strangely enough, such an efficient health care system, designed to look after animals, did not have a counterpart for looking after human beings. There were the government run dispensaries, in different villages, and private medical practitioners. Neither of them provided a satisfactory health service to the villagers. The former displayed a bureaucratic indifference and the latter excessive greed. Consequently, the villagers often stated that from a medical point of view they, the human beings, were not as important as their animals. When their babies fell ill they suffered or died, but so far as the animals were concerned, there was always very efficient veterinary assistance available for them.

Remarks of that nature often embarrassed the veterinary staff of Amul. Finally, after years of examination of various alternatives, in 1972 it produced a health programme for training medical workers in each village to be able to provide a health service based on a linkage of medical resources. Such a service was then linked with the network of milk cooperatives in the district. The two crucial problems for the implementation of this programme were funds and a medical executive who could work out the programme in detail and implement it.

The initial funding for the programme came from the Tribhu-vandas Foundation. Tribhuvandas Patel was one of the two principal makers of Amul, the other being the well-known Dr. Kurien. When the former retired, after three decades of distinguished service, which helped build one of the greatest milk cooperatives in the world, the grateful farmers of the district donated him a sizable sum. Tribhuvandas, in turn, donated the entire amount to the new health programme through the newly created Tribhuvandas Foundation. Then there was the financial assistance received from Amul itself, UNICEF, the British Overseas Ministry, etc. These resources were barely enough to launch the programme. After that, as we shall see, it needed its own independent sources of income to be able to sustain and expand its own programme.

The search for a medical executive, preferably a woman, proved to be far more difficult. The Foundation looked for a woman medical doctor of considerable experience who had the knack of building and operating a complex medical organisation in a district consisting of nearly one thousand villages. Moreover, the idea of linking medical resources, to be able to reach medical service wherever and whenever needed, rather than have a resident doctor in each community, which the organisation could not afford, was a new one for India. There were not very many Indian women doctors who were willing to try out an experiment of that magnitude and boldness. Furthermore, the range of problems relating to rural health care are so very complex that the Indian medical profession was just about beginning to realise how very limited had been its own training and experience. It had, therefore, come to the conclusion that the only way to learn more about those problems, apart from research, was learning by practising. Despite such a philosophical position there were very few who wanted to plunge themselves into an uncharted sea.

After a long search the Foundation was fortunate enough to get the services of a successful medical practitioner called Dr. Uma Vyas, from Bombay. Vyas had a lucrative practice in London, England, but wanted to return to India and do something for her own people. But she did not know where and how to begin. The possibility of joining the Foundation, therefore, greatly excited her. Before joining she was warned by the organisers of Amul that the new medical enterprise would tax her skill, energy and patience to the limit, and that at the end of her career she may not have much money but only the deep satisfaction of having pioneered one of the most difficult medical programmes in Indian history.

To be able to launch the programme, Vyas and her associates needed an army of women health workers, initially to be trained for a short period, but then on, to be encouraged to learn more and more about medical problems by means of a highly supervised health service. This was also to be supplemented with periodic formal training with emphasis on preventive and curative medicine, prenatal maternal and infant care, and nutrition, etc., at the Foundation headquarters. For that purpose two middle-aged women had to be selected by each village in the district. After careful interviews and shortlisting the villagers were told that only those who could be elected unanimously by them would be allowed to proceed for further training. Such a practice had to be followed so as to ensure their acceptance by the village as a whole. The two health workers were then designated as the village health worker and the village infant worker. The former was trained to diagnose and identify diseases that were common in the community and administer drugs. If the symptoms were too complicated, she was then asked to take her instruction from either the roving team of nurses, nutritionists, child development specialist, or doctors. Instructions were usually obtained by means of phone. In more difficult cases, nurses and doctors visited the patients in the village, and made their recommendation for treatment either in the village itself or for taking the patient in an ambulance to a newly-constructed hospital in the village of Karamsad near Anand.[4]

The women infant worker was trained to pay special attention to infants under five. She discussed and counselled women about child-rearing practices, nutrition, sanitation, and health care in general. She also organised day-care centres, recreational facilities for pre-schoolers and the distribution of highly nutritious snack food, called *mumri*, especially prepared by Amul to be sold at a nominal price for the infants. She kept a detailed record of their health, weight, triple vaccine, deworming, etc., and also kept a record of the women in the fertility group so as to persuade them to consider the possibility of leproscopy after the birth of their second child. Together both the health workers kept accounts of the cost of the entire health scheme.

For the medical service each family was expected to pay Rs.10 per year, which is under a dollar. So far as the salary of the health workers was concerned, it was shared by the village milk cooperative and the Foundation.[5] The village milk cooperative charged that amount on a proportionate basis to its shareholders at the time of their annual bonus.

Within seven years of its establishment in 1979, the Foundation was able to reach close to three hundred villages out of one thousand in the district. As could be expected, its work proved to be the toughest in the first few villages. As the organisers gained experience, certain adjustments had to be made to the initial proposals. But once they were done, the Foundation moved with great swiftness. One of the reasons for its rapid expansion was the dedication of its entire health personnel from Vyas downwards. They all were deeply aware of the fact that they were implementing a unique health service which would benefit the poor in the district. Then there was the highly efficient network of cooperative dairying organised by Amul in all the villages of the district. For a number of villagers, Amul was the source of nearly half of their income. Consequently, without its organisational facilities, and also financial help, the Foundation would not have been able to get its health scheme off the ground. So great was the importance of the economic dimension that the Foundation itself started helping the women of the villages to market their handicrafts. This further endeared the Foundation and its medical personnel to the villagers.

An average Indian village has a variety of competing medical facilities, no matter how very limited, available to its various economic and cultural groups. These include, among others, the *Dai* (midwife), Ayurvedic, Unani, Homoeopathy, Naturopathy, quacks, witch doctors, the gods and goddesses of health, all these over and above practitioners of western medicine. The new scheme had thus to operate within the givens of the rival schools and approaches to human health. To be able to penetrate such a complex health terrain of rural India required utmost tact, sensitivity, and coexistential tolerance.

Let us now briefly look at the problems which the medical personnel at the Foundation faced. From time to time the senior medical personnel at the Foundation went through its own agonising process of reappraisal. Their concerns ranged from the unfamiliarity with the problems of health in rural areas, about which their own medical schools from which they had graduated had told them precious little, to how to provide more training to the health personnel working under their supervision. They were aware of the fact that the village-level health workers knew more about the social and cultural problems which impinge on health, but lacked sufficient medical knowledge and training to be able to act effectively or even cautiously. Then there was the central issue of whether the health network and linkage – whereby medical workers of different levels and training were linked with the headquarters where full-fledged doctors were available – was the best possible solution for the health problems of the district.

Even the most highly-trained personnel at the Foundation felt that their own training was based on the assumption that the facilities, equipment, and standard of living which exists in the countries of the west are a must for any good programme of health anywhere. Since leaving medical school, and while practising their profession in urban centres, they were inclined, and forced by circumstances, to question those assumptions. Moreover, the very nature of health problems, and even diseases, were very different in rural communities from what their textbooks and medical school training had told them. Consequently, most of them confessed that they were relearning, and even retooling, their own skill and craft while faced with problems of health in rural India. Even such a major area as tropical medicine was dealt with in a cursory fashion by their training.

Then there were others who felt that the medical problems of society could not be tackled in isolation from other wider social problems, and that medical problems needed a kind of holistic approach within which health becomes an integral part of other social problems. Consequently, you could not touch the health problems of rural India in isolation from several other problems which stand in a causal relationship with them.

There was also a controversy over the problem of the pre-cedence of preventive medicine over the curative. The curative aspect of their efforts received far more attention than the preventive, which involved long-term efforts and slow results.

But the most agonising question for them was whether they, the highly trained medical personnel, were giving enough medical training to their village level women health workers or not. How far, they asked, were they justified in allowing those health workers to administer powerful drugs with a training which was below the standard of three months prescribed by the World Health Organisation?

The very fact that those problems were raised and extensively discussed by the personnel revealed a heightened sensitivity, concern and a determination to reappraise, constantly, what they were engaged in, and to seek solutions to them as they went along.

The Foundation itself was built on the philosophy that, given all the limitation of having to work in rural India, you have to take, somewhere, the pragmatic first step, and then evaluate and improvise, and learn from your own experiences as you go along. The only alternative to a fully-fledged medical programme, or several fully-trained medical personnel for every rural community, none of which it could afford, was to build a health network and linkage of medical personnel consisting of village level health workers, nurses, and doctors, and to make their services available with reference to the urgency of the situation. Under such a system the village level health worker looks after the routine problems of health, and nurses and doctors look after the more complicated ones. While such a linkage system seems to work towards the dilution of medical attention and care, it has, in actual practice, been able to come to grips with a large number of health problems in rural communities which would otherwise have remained unattended.

Let us now briefly examine the experiences of village level health workers in this new system of medical linkage.[6] Those workers, as mentioned earlier, came through a competitive process of selection, by the senior medical personnel, and then election in their own communities. Such a competitive process by its very nature was likely to hurt the feelings of unsuccessful candidates and their families. Consequently, the Foundation took great pains to emphasise the unanimous nature of final selection from among those who were shortlisted.

In such a competition, the caste and religion of various candidates also played an important part. Since upper-caste women would hesitate to go to lower-caste homes, and lower-caste women would have problems of their acceptance by the community. The Foundation's choice, as far as possible, was for the women from the middle strata of village society. But there was no hard and fast rule. The Foundation, in fact, was able to recruit some very able and dedicated women from the two ends of the social hierarchy as its health workers. Middle-aged women, with grown-up children and less household responsibilities, between 35 and 45 years, some of them widows, divorcees, or deserted women belonging to the middle rungs of the village society, often made ideal health workers.

After their training at the headquarters, those health workers had to face the moment of truth in their own communities. Initially all of them were jeered at as "doctors", meaning quacks. What finally rehabilitated them after a trying period were the visits by senior medical personnel. Such visits gave importance to the newly trained on their home ground. Then there were the usual agonising first few days, worrying about who from the village would visit them for health services first. Fortunately for those women health workers, a large part of their responsibilities also consisted of identifying the obvious cases of tuberculosis, malnutrition, stomach upsets, colds, malaria, leprosy, etc., and reporting them to the nurses and doctors at the headquarters. Then there was the responsibility of collecting and keeping records of women in the fertility group, the number of children each of them had, and preparing a list of those who could be considered for leproscopy. There was also the responsibility of keeping a record of the weights of children and the distribution of *mumri* for a nominal amount of one cent per serving per child.[7]

When it finally came to facing the patients, the health workers often had a difficult task on their hands. Ailing children who were brought to them were often in the state of advanced illness. That is because their parents had already tried a few family or neighbour advised remedies, and only then were their children brought to the medical workers. And if the ailments of those children were cured by means of medicine given by the health workers then they had instant recognition and legitimacy. The other route, a bit slower, was through advice on nutrition and the steady increase in the weight of the children. After that the whole family and its neighbours were ready for medical assistance.

By and large the women health workers became the health helpers of the poorer sections of their village. The relatively well-off villagers continued to get their medical aid from the fully-fledged private medical practitioners. Even within the poorer strata the health worker could provide help only to those who asked for it.

The most effective breaks for the health workers came when they were able to come out with their curative success by means of medication that they themselves were allowed to administer. The same was true of their effective dressing and healing of injuries. Finally, their medical credentials were considered to have been fully recognised by the community when their help and advice was sought on emergencies, possibly at night.

Several health workers whom I interviewed, some of them repeatedly, and also watched at work in their respective villages, spoke of the extraordinarily tough experiences after the training at the Foundation. Since every new trainee routinely went through such experiences, the Foundation called on the veterans among them to narrate their first few experiences to those who were about to be launched in their own communities. Over a period of more than seven years, since the beginning of the programme, not a single health worker gave up out of sheer demoralisation. Some who gave up had their personal reasons such as their own possible second marriage, after widowhood, or some other family circumstances. The veterans among them beamed with a lot of confidence. They clamoured for more training and a greater share in health responsibilities. A whole new world had opened up for them. After their initial problems, they had acquired a great faith in their own ability to help the people of their own villages. Such a newly-acquired, and gradually recognised, skill gave them a new status. Gone were the days when the villager jeered at them by calling them "doctors". They were now seen as the most vital link in the health structure which the Foundation had established. And what is more, through them the poor of the village, in 336 (1988) rural communities already covered by this programme, could for the first time obtain, after paying a very small fee, the best health care and attention that one could possibly get in the district. There was yet another message in it for the village itself, and that is by training some of their own people, possibly women, they could get a part of those resources for education and social services which are monopolised by the towns and their inhabitants. Above all, there was also a lesson in self-help; the people of the village could be trained to look after a part of their own health problems.

NEW ATTITUDE TO WOMEN AT WORK

One of the major problems in rural India is the under-utilisation of the available labour. Agricultural crops do not keep all those involved in them occupied throughout the year. This is also true of farms which have relatively easy access to water all the year round. Depending upon the nature and number of crops, the average farmer remains occupied with farm work from four to nine months a year.

Rural women, in the majority of cases, after household work in the morning, usually join their husbands in the fields, especially during peak agricultural seasons. Consequently, barring peak seasons, they too have spare time at their disposal. This is despite the fact that they have to forage for fuel wood, bring drinking water from a distance, look after the animals, and attend to a number of things around the house.

Lastly, unmarried girls, who as a rule are not allowed by their parents to continue in schools after puberty, help their mothers in domestic work and in looking after their siblings. So far as boys are concerned, not only do they spend more time in schools but they also regularly assist their parents on the farm. Consequently, men, women, boys and girls, all have different proportion of their time under-utilised.

Any economic enterprise of an industrial variety in rural India which aims at utilising the unused proportion of human labour, has to address itself to the question of what kind of unused labour is available and to what particular use can it be put. The two categories of labour, apart from seasonally employed males, are the married women who are available for a part of the time, and unmarried girls between the ages of twelve and eighteen who are, or can be, available for a full day's work.

Unmarried girls in Indian villages are considered to *belong* to villages where they would be married. This is because of strictly defined and enforced circles of marriages. There are a strictly catalogued number of villages, as we saw earlier, to which girls of a particular caste, in a specific region, can be married, and another list of villages from where brides are brought. Such endogamous matrimonial arrangements are strictly enforced by most caste councils. Consequently, depending on the customs of various regions, and the standards of matrimony imposed by various social groups within them, the girls of the village, in order to maintain the purity of blood of the progeny, do not marry in the village of their birth.

Before the girls go to their in-laws, parents develop an ambivalent attitude towards them. On the one hand, parents want to meet as many of their requirements as possible, not knowing what kind of future their daughters will get in their in-laws' house. On the other hand, they keep reminding their daughters to make do with whatever they possibly can, and thereby prepare themselves for an uncertain future. Then as parents they also keep reminding themselves, again and again, not to get too attached to their daughters. Since *beti to parai* (daughters belong to others), one day they would have to let them go. Conversely, since *beta to apna*, (boys are our own), they get special privileges, longer education, more and better food, etc.

In days gone by, parents used to hesitate to put their unmarried daughters to work. It was considered to be socially demeaning to live off a daughter's income. It was believed that you only give things to your daughter and not take anything from her, least of all her income. But over the years such attitudes have changed. In such a change what has helped is the realisation that the daughters will pick up new skills or a trade which will be useful to them, in case they are required to depend on their own resources in the event of widowhood, desertion or the breakdown of marriage.

It was such a change in attitude to work for women which was effectively utilised by a medium-size food processing and canning industry, called VAFA, in the heart of Kaira district. VAFA was started by Savita Amin, a highly-trained educator and a Columbia University alumnus turned industrialist. She was also deeply involved in a number of social work activities, ranging from organising schools for pre-schoolers and the handicapped, a house for destitute and separated women, an organisation for middle-class women wanting to do voluntary health work in hospitals, etc. Her latest venture is in the field of the assembly of small parts by middle-class women at an hourly wage for the industrial units of Baroda. They make roughly around two to three hundred rupees per month.

VAFA is a well-managed industrial unit on the family's ancestral property in the village of Vatadara. The farm employed men and women from the surrounding villages, especially during peak seasons, but there was not enough work to go around. Amin, therefore, decided to start a canning factory and called it Vatadara Farm, in short VAFA, to give employment to women with spare time and also teach them new skills, hygiene, general education, family planning and child rearing in general. Moreover, in the evenings, after meals, VAFA arranged a number of games, *bhajans* (devotional music), plays by roving companies, and films. Consequently VAFA became not only a source of year-round employment, but also of education and community entertainment.

Moreover, as a processing factory, VAFA needed large quantities of fruits and vegetables which it could not grow on its own farms. Consequently it started involving farmers in neighbouring villages in producing them. For that purpose VAFA supplied improved seeds, seedlings, techniques of cultivation, the supervision of crops and, above all, an assured market. The villages in the neighbourhood, as a result, started registering considerable economic growth.

Depending on the season, VAFA employed two to three hundred full-time workers in its fruit and vegetable canning unit. The bulk of them were women and unmarried girls. The few men who were employed were in charge of heavy work, or office work.

The rural women workforce of VAFA was largely drawn from the middle and lower strata of the rural society. A large number of them came from the Kshatriya and Vaghari castes. Economically speaking, these women came from families with small to very small land holdings. Consequently, the steady additional income which these women brought in was of great help to their families. Within the workforce there were also a few upper-caste Patidars and Venkars, the ex-untouchables.[8]

Men and women worked in mixed situations. The same is true of women of different social origins. Work for them cut across gender and ethnic divisions. Unmarried girls earned up to about Rs.150 and women and men earned up to about Rs.300 a month. These amounts, as year-round supplementary incomes in Indian villages, are considered to be substantial. Then there were part-time workers who were also able to supplement their family income.

The additional income provided by VAFA is thus most welcome to rural communities. To some extent it had even ucceeded in discouraging migrations to industrial centres from heir surrounding rural communities by providing employment.

The success of VAFA was largely due to its ability to address ts efforts to the pressing problems of rural communities in its eighbourhood. The most acute problem, as stated earlier, was he under-utilisation of the available labour. What VAFA had herefore done was to build its industrial unit to be able to use uch labour. And through this it also inculcated a number of ew approaches to agriculture, health, hygiene, family planning nd education in general.

Let us now briefly examine some of the implications of the pportunity for work provided by VAFA, especially to girls efore marriage. Girls, before they get married, get a work span f about two to six years in Indian villages. As stated earlier, ntil a few years ago it was considered to be unthinkable to send nmarried girls to work in rural areas. This was true of a large umber of social groups in rural society. To that the lower castes, vhich constituted the poorest of the poor, were an exception.

As a rule, daughters could help in household work and then o out and help their parents on their farms. But to put them to vork somewhere else for wages was considered to be socially ndesirable. It was also considered to be risky for fear of lopement, pregnancy or unkind gossip jeopardising the chance f their marriage. Traditionally speaking, therefore, parents in ural areas, no matter how very needy they were, desisted from utting their unmarried girls to work despite the urgent need or it.

Middle-class parents in urban centres, however, were the first o concede, gradually and grudgingly, the right of unmarried irls to work in offices, schools, banks, etc. Such a privilege was ot enjoyed by their counterparts in rural communities.

In that respect what VAFA achieved was a significant social reakthrough. It not only succeeded in persuading parents to end their daughters to work but also succeeded in getting their vould-be in-laws to approve of it. This is because most of the nmarried girls at VAFA were engaged to be married. While hey waited for their marriage, because of the legal barrier to arly marriage, their would-be in-laws, located in different illages, through their own gossip and information circuit, nvariably had a clear idea of the activities of the girls. So far s VAFA was concerned it was very rare that the would-be in-laws sent messages disapproving of the young girls going to work.

Apart from the additional income which the parents earned which was then saved for expenses on marriage, the daughter learnt new skills, the discipline of outdoor work, work in mixed situations, etc., which was bound to be useful to them later on in life when, after bringing up their family, they would look for work as an additional source of income. Simultaneously, the unmarried girls at work were gradually chipping away at the bulwark of the traditional social constraint to work itself. They were increasingly making work before marriage acceptable to their own tradition-bound society. What is more, the bulk of the unmarried girls at VAFA were of the Kshatriya community which was considered to be socially most conservative and backward. Consequently, the change introduced by opportunities at VAFA were considered to be most welcome by their own younger leadership.

For the girls working at VAFA, the possibility of finding similar work after marriage in other villages were slim. Nevertheless, they were in a better position to work in the scores of smaller industrial units which were springing up in a number of villages in the district. Through such training, women in rural areas, as in the urban areas before them, were beginning to acquire a new role for themselves. Wherever a suitable opportunity presented itself, they emerged as the cobreadwinners for their families. Their cobreadwinner status was rarely recognised when they worked side-by-side with their husbands on the family farm. But if they worked for wages elsewhere then their income from there instantly became a noticeable additional income.

Thus, in rural India, the attitude to women at work was gradually and imperceptibly changing. New opportunities for work, and semi-skilled work, together with economic necessity and a slight relaxation in the traditional constraints on women at work, had opened up a new access to paid outdoor work for women. What now stood in the way of women going to work was less and less a matter of traditional constraint and more a matter of the availability of suitable work in terms of the block of time they could take out for such work. Rural poverty and unutilised or semi-utilised labour resource in rural India made new opportunities for work for women hard to come by.

DEMANDING UNION AND PUBLIC POLICY PROTECTION

In practically all societies, developed or developing, women's labour is exploited and underpaid. In the bulk of them there are no adequate safeguards for a fair wage, decent treatment, or a share in property. According to UN statistics women are paid only ten per cent of all wages and salaries, and only one per cent of whatever they get is owned by them.[9]

Among women in general the plight of women who are self-employed in either the urban or rural sectors of the bulk of the developing countries has been much worse. In most cases they do not even have the protection of their own menfolk. Consequently, over and above the exploitation of their labour, they are often considered to be objects of derision, verbal and physical abuse, and exploitation. Traditionally speaking, a large number of people in those societies have got used to the practice of getting their services without due regard to the question of the fairness of wages offered to them. In the absence of their own organisation, or of a public policy governing the rate of remuneration, or strict implementation of it if there is one in existence, self-employed women often end up getting the most inhuman treatment at the hands of the people they do business with. This is particularly true of women who have recently migrated to urban centres from rural areas in search of work and livelihood.

In the burgeoning textile capital of India, namely Ahmedabad, self-employed women presented an incredible picture of exploitation and indignity. In that city an average woman vegetable vendor borrowed Rs.50 from a money-lender every morning, bought vegetables from wholesale dealers, rented a weight scale and pushcart, spent the whole day hawking vegetables door to door and at street corners, repaid the money-lender Rs.55, paid rent for the weight scale and pushcart, and at the end of the day she would be lucky if she could save Rs.10 for her entire day's labour. In the process of making her living she was also harassed by bribe-extracting street corner policemen and market goons.

The Annual Report of SEWA (1986) listed 103 cases of police harassment of female vegetable vendors. But it also mentioned that with the help of SEWA's legal services, 45 women were able to recover the bribes which they were forced to pay the police.

The same was true of women who bought rags and made quil
covers with the help of rented sewing machines, or junksmith
who bought discarded metal clippings and with hired tools made
tumblers and containers, the pushcart pullers who transported
goods, block printers, or those who made *padadams* and made
agarbattis (incense sticks). They all borrowed money every day
and, after paying off whatever they owed to others, they took
home very little. In most cases this went on for generations, from
mother to daughter.

Most of these women were migrants from rural areas. They
often came from the lower strata of society and were illiterate
They had husbands who either did not work or had deserted
them. A number of these women also had dependent children
Whenever they mustered sufficient courage to say something to
either the money-lenders or the middlemen, they were made to
shut up after a lot of obscenities or were even physically assaulted

To provide protection to such women, whose labour was a
source of income for money-lenders, well entrenched middlemen
market toughs and socially undesirable elements, was indeed a
difficult job. And the person who succeeded in providing it
despite many problems, was Ela Bhatt, the founder of an
organisation called the Self-Employed Women's Association
(SEWA). This is her story.

Bhatt had several years of experience as a trade union organiser
in the textile city of Ahmedabad. Consequently, she tried very
hard to persuade her union colleagues to extend its organisational
protection to self-employed women in the textile metropolis
Neither her colleagues nor the textile commissioner, who regula-
ted union activities on behalf of the government, welcomed the
idea in the beginning. The main problem was whether those
self-employed women could be considered, technically speaking,
as workers or not. Bhatt's own colleagues were apprehensive of
the possibility of such a vaguely-defined group of women workers
weakening, in the long run, the trade union movement itself.[10]
But then there was the other side to the trade union. This one,
i.e. the Textile Labour Association (earlier called the Majdoor
Mahajan), was founded by none other than Mahatma Gandhi.
And as could be expected he was offering the protection of a
union to all those who needed it the most. Finally, it was agreed
that SEWA would be allowed to affiliate itself to the umbrella

organisation. In 1972, SEWA registered itself as union of self-employed women.[11]

Bhatt's success, however, was short-lived. In 1980 when she got involved in another burning issue, i.e. reserved seats in medical institutions for students from ex-untouchable castes, she was thrown out of the union itself for having taken sides.[12] By that time Bhatt had emerged as a prominent organiser of SEWA with a lot of respect for her dedicated work throughout the country. Consequently, she was now in a position to work on her own.

Since its inception, SEWA was able to enrol a membership of 20,811 women (1986). Those women were most enthusiastic, deeply devoted and grateful members. SEWA had divided its membership into three broad categories: home-based producers, who got their raw materials and made *bidis* or tobacco leaf cigarettes, *agarbattis*, garments, small furniture, block prints and handicrafts; small vendors who sold vegetables, fish, spices and other consumer goods; and labourers who provided various kinds of services such as cart-pulling, headloading, scrap-metal collecting, rags and waste-paper picking, etc.

Each of these categories came to have its own leader who understood the peculiar problem of that trade. To be economically effective SEWA needed their input, direction and resourcefulness. Such leaders were elected by the membership within a particular trade. They then became the members of SEWA's decision-making body. Over and above this SEWA got its own research done with the help of the graduate students and faculty of Gujarat University in Ahmedabad. This was particularly helpful when it needed fresh ideas and approaches to marketing.

Each member of SEWA gets the services of its three basic organisations. They are the SEWA Union, SEWA Bank, and SEWA Mahila Trust. The union provides a set-up for normal union activities, the bank provides banking and credit facilities, and the trust provides facilities for legal aid, social security, training in new skills, and education in general.[13]

SEWA as a union had its own share of problems in fighting for fair wages for pushcart pullers, headloaders and others in odd jobs. For one thing, people who were used to getting services at self-fixed wages, or wages fixed by tough middlemen, were indeed unhappy to have to part with the extra cash. Moreover, they did not expect *women*, and above all illiterate labour class women, to talk to them in the language of a union, with its solidarity and collective clout. On their part the women themselves took some time to make a difficult psychological transition from a docile receiver of whatever was given to them to an insistent, union-quoting, and, in some cases, a talking-back bargainer. Quite often their leaders went along with them to make sure that the cash received was appropriate, given the haggling, swearing and the rough atmosphere of the labour market in general.

The employers of women also took some time to come to terms with the new version of union card waving, instruction quoting, and much less bashful employees. The employers grumbled and cursed the union for having poisoned the minds of illiterate women. But in the course of time they had to come to terms with the new reality.

In the trial of strength, to extract or deny the increased wage, the unionised woman had a distinct edge. She knew that her leaders, the union office, and the lawyers, were there to back up her demands. And so far as the employer was concerned, he had nightmares of how the unions, which in the textile city of Ahmedabad could cripple mighty big business houses, were going to treat him.

SEWA also succeeded in persuading the various levels of government, the Planning Commission, and the International Labour Organisation, together with various other international agencies, of the need to broaden the definition of "workers" to be able to include self-employed women. It pointed out to them the precarious nature of their work and the manner of their exploitation in the absence of legislation governing their wage structure and conditions of work.

SEWA's greatest single achievement was in the field of establishing a bank for credit facilities for the self-employed women who often paid exorbitant interest to money-lenders. In 1974 it established the Mahila Sahakari Bank (Women's Cooperative Bank, popularly known as the SEWA Bank), the only one of its kind in India.[14]

By 1983, more than 18,000 women had opened their accounts in the bank.[15] Since the bulk of those women were illiterate, the problem of signature was overcome by means of thumb prints and photographs on bank passbooks. Simultaneously, the bank conducted a campaign of teaching women how to sign their names. There too it had a phenomenal success. Women depositers often left behind their passbooks so as not to divulge the information regarding their growing bank balance.

Within three years of its existence, the bank advanced loans to 6,000 women at 4 per cent, which was one-third of what other banks charged, and very much less than what the money-lenders charged. This it could do because of its ability to use some funds earmarked for women's development. Surprisingly enough, there were very few cases of default in the loan repayment. In a short time women began to own their own tools of trade, pushcarts, sewing machines, corner stalls, etc.

The bank was entirely managed by women and it was not possible to remain unmoved by the enthusiasm, chatter, screams and laughter of the hoards of women clients who moved in and out of it. The jubilation was there not always because of the growing bank balance and the periodic interest which it earned, but also because of a sense of achievement which till a few years ago was inconceivable.

SEWA now wanted its members to move on to different fields by acquiring new skills. Consequently, it had arranged training programmes in the fields of bamboo work, sophisticated block-printing, and sewing, weaving, carpentry, plumbing, radio repair, etc. These new skills are now opening up new markets and possibilities for women.[16] SEWA has also succeeded in establishing its chapters in different parts of the country and thereby is able to tackle similar problems of women elsewhere.

Let us now briefly examine the work done by SEWA in rural areas. In 1977, while still a part of the larger union, SEWA, gropingly, got involved in women in rural communities. In a sense its own membership, despite its location in the city, had a strong rural connection. In most cases its membership had come from women who had migrated to the periphery of the city in search of work. They had, therefore, sensitised SEWA to the problems of women who were left behind in the villages.

Apart from the steady flow of surplus and unemployed labourers into urban centres from rural areas in search of work, periods of drought and famine had often increased the volume of such a flow. The women among such new arrivals in towns were particularly the objects of ruthless exploitation by urban middlemen and employers.

While year after year, politicians, planners, economists and bureaucrats talked about keeping the surplus rural labour force in the villages, precious little was done by them to hold them there. So far as SEWA was concerned, it had decided to concentrate on villages which constituted the labour resource area of the sprawling industrial metropolis of Ahmedabad. From such areas men had initially migrated to the city in search of work leaving behind their womenfolk in the villages to follow later. The men in the city had hoped to do well enough to be able to bring their families. Such hopes did not always materialise. In the course of time even their remittances and visits back to the villages became fewer and fewer.

The women back in the villages lived below the poverty line and in perpetual fear and anxiety as to the health and safety of their men. Then there was the constant fear of the presence of loose women, floating around shantytowns, rendering services of all kinds, and virtually taking over the place of wives. Such anxieties had made women back in the villages shadows of their former selves, sinking deeper and deeper in gloom and poverty. Such villages were roughly within the radius of forty to sixty kilometers from the city of Ahmedabad, too far for men to cycle to, and too expensive to go to and return by train or bus too often.

SEWA adopted a number of such villages for its programme of training women in new skills. These villages were Devdholera, Metal, Chhabasar, Baldana, etc. SEWA wanted to teach them home-based crafts, the products of which could be easily marketed in the city. Along with SEWA also came the National Dairy Development Board (NDDB) to give a helping hand in stimulating cooperative dairying in those villages with the help of loans for buying milch animals.[17]

Both these organisations soon found out that their problems were tougher than they had anticipated. Prolonged anxiety, insecurity, and the fear of the future as wives had drained of whatever little motivation or energy there was in the women who were left behind in the villages. The last thing on their mind, at this stage, was how to improve their own economic condition. Unlike the city, where self-employed women after their ruthless exploitation were prepared to fight back, the women of these villages were not very sure where they would be in the future. The occasional visits of their husbands, the big talk of life in the city, and the promise of taking them along had made these women uncertain as to their own movement.

So far as the milk cooperative was concerned, it had a shaky start. Since women, separated from their men at work in the city, could not attend to their animals as they should have, the milk productivity of the animals, bought with the help of subsidy or loans, started dwindling. Moreover, it was difficult for those rural communities – with their women at unease, and few unemployed or old men left behind – to supervise effectively the work of the milk cooperative. Consequently, the unscrupulous office-bearers of those village milk cooperatives had a free hand with the finances of those organisations.

The attempt to teach new crafts to the village women also had a poor start, but later on it picked up to become a phenomenal success. The first group of women to respond to the scheme to teach new skills were from social groups which were traditionally involved in weaving and basket making. Later on twenty Venkar families (weaver caste) were retrained in the modern art of wool-weaving. Their success in marketing what they designed and crafted under the supervision of skilled teachers attracted other women to join in. In the winter in 1984, Devdholera, one of the villages, marketed what came to be known, nationally, as the famous *Devdholera shawls*. Those were instantly sold out. English national dailies even wrote articles on them. Orders started pouring in, much beyond the capacity of a small village. Overnight Devdholera was put on the map of India.

On the human side SEWA not only helped the women of those villages to make a significant breakthrough in the handicraft market, and thereby earn an additional income, but also to pick up the pieces of their own lives after the migration of their men to urban centres.

SEWA, by means of its several activities, thus put across to the women that they, a disadvantaged group in a traditional society, could help themselves a great deal in seeking a way out of the tough situation in which they found themselves, and that, in the final analysis, they would have to help themselves. Male reformers and female sympathisers can go only a part of the way. They can rouse the conscience of the society, exhort women to get actively involved in various social activities, and provide institutional guarantees and policy provisions. But all these will need takers and utilisers of all that has been provided. Moreover, even when provisions are made in law and policy, they cannot guarantee their uncheated or untruncated utilisation. For that women themselves will have to act and make sure that they get what has been professed and provided for.

SEWA, by means of its own regenerative processes, was thus engaged in transforming a section of women into different shades of activists. As activists, the women were also becoming aware of the need for the collective utilisation of opportunities provided for them, rather than merely looking after their own interests as individuals.

Moreover, as a women's collectivity, SEWA was able to build a secular organisation, regardless of ethnic origin, to achieve the basic goal that was common to them, namely fair treatment and policy protection for women to be able to overcome traditional disadvantages. While women with their social and occupational background functioned as segments within SEWA, their overall loyalty to the organisation did not diminish because of their segmental links. This proved to be a boon to those women who, along with the legal union umbrella of SEWA, also wanted to belong to their own traditional occupational groups. Under these circumstances, the metal scrap workers, dyers, block printers, rag pickers, etc., remained firmly based in their traditional occupational groups, while at the same time they built yet another overarching group, with its added clout, and that was SEWA. Such an achievement helped SEWA to have its own solidarity without forcing women out of their traditional-cum-occupational groups.

In its regenerative process SEWA thus kept intact the sense of security which is associated with a kingroup pursuing its own trade for generations, and yet welded such a group into a wider collectivity to be able to seek the protection and dignity which the law could provide. SEWA thus became a secular group consisting of many traditional occupational groups within it. Its regenerative process had thus safely insulated various groups within it and thereby spared them the possible traumatic shock of an outright merger into an impersonal collectivity.

Let us now examine the implications of the work which SEWA had undertaken for women in general. Out of the four instances of regenerative processes examined in this chapter to prepare the women of rural and urban communities for a new role and scope for work, the effort of SEWA was the boldest. It was designed to seek protection for women from both society and its tradition-ridden, and often insensitive, male component.

In launching its own regenerative activity, SEWA did not want to overlook the fact that ultimately what counts in getting one's fair share and rewards is one's own strength within the various social equations and situations on the one hand, and the pressure put on policy-makers *before* they make policies, on the other. The former led it to resort to a time-honoured solution of unionisation, generating its own collective clout, solidarity, and legal resources to be able to manipulate the social and economic forces of the market place. The latter led to lobbying in the corridors of power, i.e. the legislatures, Planning Commission, and various ministries. In 1986, Bhatt herself was awarded the title of Padma Bhushan and was also nominated to the Rajya Sabha, the upper house of Indian Parliament, giving her added access to influence policy making.

For too long the leaders of Indian social and religious reform movements, nationalist leaders, and voluntary workers adopted the method of changing the attitude of men and society by appealing to their reason and conscience. While that was necessary, what SEWA did not want to forget was that women, ultimately, were as strong as the organisation they were able to build to protect themselves and also effectively lobby for social legislation and public policy to be able to seek legal redress. That law provided an overarching umbrella within which, through their organisation and solidarity, they had to secure what was rightfully theirs.

The founder of SEWA herself came from the trade union movement of western India. And in her lifetime she had seen how industrial workers were able to obtain a fair share of wages, bonuses, better working conditions, etc. through their unionised efforts. Up to a point, given the nature of the work of women in certain segments of the economy, such an approach and solution was possible for women's problems. But that is as far as it could go. Then there were women in other segments of the economy who needed different approaches and strategies. A correct understanding of what those situations were and what strategies would work there was therefore most vital.

SOME GENERAL OBSERVATIONS

In the foregoing instances of regenerative processes – regenerating
a new outlook and a renewed sense of usefulness for women,
providing them with the scope for new social roles, and attacking,
by way of the cumulative effect of all these efforts, the gross mass
of traditional relationships and attitudes which had tied down
women to positions of disadvantages – what the elite women did
was to begin where the social reformers and nationalist leaders
of the last and this century had left off. They in fact went much
beyond the efforts of the early reformers. They actually prepared
and enabled women to play new roles in society and take on
new challenges and responsibilities, a task which the early mass
mobilisation of women could not address itself to. Their enabling
efforts prepared women for yet another step to be taken by them,
i.e. that of self-involvement in a variety of social, economic and
political pursuits. The various processes that were implicit in
the regenerative efforts of the elite women did not always take
place in the same area, nor related to the same individuals, nor
indeed systematically phased in one after another. Nevertheless,
they took place in the same or adjoining districts with a proximity
close enough to inspire emulative efforts in an ever-widening
circle of women.

While elites play an important part in all societies, their role
in a developing country like India is a special one. This is
because apart from being an elite-oriented and elite-led society,
India faced the peculiar problem of the establishment of various
new public institutions, after her independence, without the prior
or the simultaneous growth of the political capacity of her people
to be able to deal with those institutions, and the people who
occupied public office within them. Such institutions, in almost
all walks of life, are established much in advance of the
commensurate growth of the political capacity of her people.
Nehru and various constitutional lawyers, who were in charge
of establishing the legal and political institutions of India,
implicitly believed that once those institutions were created, the
citizens of India would automatically grow in their stature and
capacity to be able to utilise the various provisions for rights,
social equality and justice.

Such confidence was misplaced. Realistically speaking,
between such provisions and the human political capacity to use

them, there were not only gaps but deeply entrenched traditional constraints.[18] Such gaps and constraints further reinforced the need for elites not only to mobilise people but also to help them to realise, in practice, the fruits of those provisions. What was true of the Indian situation, generally, was also true of the work which the elites could do for women. In specific areas they took on the function of preparing their women followers to realise in practice those provisions within the newly-created institutions, and later on in various opportunities created by the constantly revised public policy. But in the case of women they also had to help their followers to rise against the conventional attitudes and practices, largely favouring men, which had been followed without question for centuries. In that sense it fell on the elite women to build the social capacity of their followers to be able to overcome traditional constraints and also go on to claim what had been provided by public institutions and policies for women in general.

The elite women, in their efforts to prepare their women followers to take on new roles and functions for themselves, had also created a few actual and potential problems. They had viewed the role of rural women with reference to their own vision and understanding, with a built-in urban middle-class bias and perspective of how certain new activities should be undertaken by them. While in the initial stage such an elite-indicated direction was inevitable, the model provided by them could have been taken as the surest and unalterable guide for the followers. The *margdarshan* (guidance), as the women of the region called it, given by the elite women helped their followers to cut through the frightening maze of constraints, with "dont's" boldly written on them, and helped them to plunge into new situations. The success of such a *margdarshan* has to be judged with reference to what the followers made of their own experiences in practice. Did they need such guidance all the time? Or did they grow in their own social and political capacity to look after themselves after the initial mobilisation and *margdarshan*? Those were the crucial questions.

All the instances of elite women's regenerative efforts identified in this chapter, are so recent that no judgement can be passed on what happened to their women followers, in terms of their own self-development, in the post-initiation and guidance period. If what the health workers experienced is any guide, they, the veterans of the initial experience, partially take on, as we saw earlier, the role of those who give far more effectively and realistically the next instalment of *margdarshan*. Similarly the SEWA trained leaders in different trades draw in new potential leaders and train them on their own.

The larger role of preparing women to play a variety of new roles was to underline the supreme importance of self-development through self-involvement and thereby the breaking out of a traditional mould which had placed them in a continuing position of disadvantage. Some of the new roles required training, others a change of attitude and a little bit of daring. For too long, women in rural India, by silently accepting the traditional prescriptions of what they can and cannot do, had lost their own individual initiative to explore what else was within their reach without wrecking their own family life or incurring the wrath of their elders. Each successive step towards such an assertion, taking on some more unconventional roles, as we saw in this chapter, convinced them of the possible acceptance of some more steps by people around them.

There were, nevertheless, few areas where neither a prior training nor *margdarshan* from the elite women was possible. And that was the area of their self-involvement in the participatory processes of the newly-created economic and political institutions. As we shall see in Chapter 4, the women who tried such an involvement had different degrees of success. They had far more success in the new economic institutions than in the political. And within the latter when they were graduating from an unmixed situation, of all female, to a mixed situation of male and female, the test of their enhanced capacity was about the severest. And still that remained the ultimate goal for their regenerative processes whereby women would learn to participate in decisions which affect everybody's lives rather than those of women only.

Before we leave this section, one final point needs to be mentioned here. And that is that all these elite women themselves benefited the most because of the liberal men either in their own families or as co-workers. Most of these women came from families which either had a social work background or had deep respect for those doing it. They did not perceive their work as against men *per se*, but against certain attitudes and practices of men and society which had put women to disadvantage.[19] At the other extreme, the women in rural India, whom the elite women trained, also had liberal-minded men as fathers, husbands, brothers, sons, or fathers-in-law to encourage them in trying out new values and roles. That was as far as their encouragement could go. After that the main work of either *margdarshan* or of acting upon it fell on the women at the two ends of the regenerating process. For women at both ends liberal men were there to stand by their side and give them moral support. But the main work of changing the values of women and introducing and training them for their possible new roles had to be done entirely by women themselves.

All the three elite women worked in close cooperation with men-led successful economic enterprises. They were more concerned with helping women, even with the help of men, than settling a score with them on gender lines.

There was, however, some difference in the women who were attracted to their regenerative efforts. While the Tribhuvandas Foundation attracted women who were social workers, young widows and deserted wives, SEWA had a large number of women who were beginning to acquire the militancy of the unions, given the harshness of their own earlier experiences, which was then moderated by the organisers.

All in all, the elite women as well as the women who followed them, without incurring gender hostility, were, in a quiet way, bringing about, in highly specific areas, some of the far-reaching changes in rural and urban communities.

4 Aspects of Economic and Political Involvement in Rural Communities

Women in rural communities in India are not just one single group but a baffling variety of several social and economic groups even within one district. Their relationship with men and their outlook on work is determined as much by the cultural values of their group as by the economic activities in which they are involved. In order to get a glimpse of the world of rural women, and of their relationship with their menfolk, we shall take into account a number of social groups within the same region spread over a few adjoining districts. Not only that, we shall also try and understand their gender relationships against the background of the recently introduced cooperative dairying and the participatory opportunities provided by it in its decision-making bodies.

While men were initially targeted by the dairy industry as traditional heads of their households, it soon found out that the new and emerging managers of the milk economy were the women. It therefore switched its various extension programmes and strategies to women as critical agents of development. Its changed policies were designed to involve more and more women in the dairy industry. The one area where it could not directly intervene was that of the formal decision-making bodies where, despite the growing importance of women, men continued to sit. And yet, within the differentiated participation by various social groups, the involvement of women in the dairy industry was continually on the increase.

Within some of the social groups, and in particular among the Adivasi or tribal communities, the gender distance between men and women being minimal, women registered a substantial or near-equal participation along with their menfolk on various decision-making bodies.

The experience of women in getting involved in either decision-making bodies or in managing public institutions was not always a pleasant one. Women of those villages where there was a mixture of several castes had some of the toughest challenges on their hands, especially when they moved from a secure all-women situation to those where there were men and women present.

Then there were certain instances where women even prevailed over men in discouraging seasonal migratory movements in search of urban employment in house building or road construction work. Together these instances constituted a complex mosaic of relationships where women were making small but steady gains in their traditional relationship with men.

The chapter is divided into the following six parts: men's domain, women's ascent; segmented gender equations and social involvements; learning to face a variety of operational problems; the bitter taste of graduating from unmixed to mixed situations; reluctant partners in seasonal migrations; and some observations on women's economic and political involvement. We shall now examine each of these points in some detail.

MEN'S DOMAIN: WOMEN'S ASCENT

In the district of Mehsana, in western India, the dairy industry, chiefly involving women, has made phenomenal progress in the last two decades. Women in several rural communities there, belonging to different social groups, have registered different degrees of involvement and a rise in importance in the industry. Such an unequal ascent of women in different communities could be attributed, as we shall see, to their special skill in rearing milch animals, to the norms of behaviour and scope of economic involvement prescribed by men, and to the interest taken by liberal-minded men in involving women in various institutions.

One of the largest milk cooperatives of India is the Dudhsagar Dairy located in the town of Mehsana. Since its establishment in 1961 it has made great strides. It has provided an income of nearly $100m (1986) to the district by way of the sale of milk and milch animals. The credit for such a remarkable achievement goes to its founder Mansinhbhai Patel, a dedicated team of dairy technologists, engineers, vets, stockmen, and, above all, a milk-producing community, consisting largely of women, who were willing to try out new ideas in cattle feeding and breeding, and to learn to improve milk productivity in general.

The district of Mehsana does not have good soil, nor good rainfall, nor even big enough rivers with irrigation potential. Consequently, for its agricultural purposes it has to depend on bore wells. In recent years, its continually increasing income from milk helped the district to invest in bore wells and thereby develop its agriculture.

Moreover, its major agricultural resources are the famous *mehsani* buffalo, well-known for its high milk yield, and an agricultural caste, the Chaudhuries, which has earned a reputation as great breeders of milch animals. Within that caste their women in particular, as we shall presently see, were mainly responsible for such an achievement.

Mansinhbhai, the founder of Dudhsagar dairy, himself belonged to the Chaudhury caste. Within the social organisation of the region, the Chaudhuries are sometimes regarded as a separate segment of the Patidar caste, and on other occasions as a distinct caste. In a number of villages in the district there is open rivalry between the Chaudhuries and the Patidars (Kadava), with the latter often claiming a hierarchical superiority over the former.

As a people the Chaudhuries, in search of higher economic and social status, have emerged as a very industrious group. The Patidars, compared to them, are considered to be more self-assured and less hard-working. Compared to the Chaudhuries, the Patidars have more land and fewer milch animals, and since income from milk has increased at a much faster rate than agricultural income in recent years, the Chaudhuries have registered a higher rate of economic development.

The other social group involved in dairying are the traditional caste of migrant keepers of animals called Rabaris. Since they have remained obsessed with the traditional ways of animal breeding, avoiding both artificial insemination and specially prepared animal feed, they have not benefited much by the recent boom in the dairy industry.

Then there are the Momens (Muslims) and Momins (Ismailis) who, along with dairying, developed a flourishing milch animal trade in the district.

In this section we shall examine the involvement of the women of most of these social groups in the dairy industry and see how they have fared, over the years, in their own rise to social and economic importance *vis-à-vis* men.

As the dairy industry expanded in Mehsana, the organisers of Dudhsagar came to realise the importance of the role of women in it. Women have always been the actual, though not formally recognised, managers of the milk economy. They look after practically all the work relating to dairying, right from feeding, scrubbing, and grazing to the milking and delivering of milk at milk coop. They have always been around when the vets examine the animals and administer treatment, including artificial insemination. However, when it comes to their participation in the various decision-making bodies relating to dairying, women often go into the background and men take over. So very widely accepted is such a practice that, barring few exceptions, women hardly protest against it.

Over the years, the vets from Dudhsagar have been in close touch with women in various rural communities. They have come to acquire a great respect for the women's role, and, in particular, that of the Chaudhury women in the dairy industry. The understanding, care and skill of the Chaudhury women in rearing animals sometimes baffles even the best in the profession.

The Chaudhury women pick up the necessary skill in looking after the animals usually from their mothers. But they do not, however, stop there. They also pick up, without much difficulty, the new techniques of feeding, animal health care, etc. from the vets. So much so that the vets often depend on those women to pick up the new ways from them and then demonstrate the new skill to others. Despite their low level of literacy, these women are very articulate, to the point of being argumentative, forward-looking and innovative. In various demonstrations arranged for backward caste women, the vets often use the services of Chaudhury women. In short, these women and their animals act as labs for vets at the practical level.

Such a perception of the usefulness of these women had so far been confined to animal breeding and milk productivity. The crisis of the late 1970s, which resulted in a short-lived milk strike, persuaded the organisers of Dudhsagar to involve them, and also other women, in various aspects of milk cooperative dairying.

That crisis was about higher prices for milk. The demand for it was launched entirely by men in seventy-nine out of twelve hundred villages in the district. The organisers of Dudhsagar argued that whatever profit the cooperative made at Mehsana was regularly paid back in the form of a bonus to the shareholders.

And so far as its own organisational expenses, along with the veterinary unit and animal feed plant were concerned, there was no scope for exercising cuts anywhere. The only possible source for an increase in the price of milk was the consumer. And that, according to the organisers, given the various market forces, was not possible.

As it was, the urban consumers of milk were pressuring the politicians to bring down the price of milk and all other agricultural products. Moreover, there were the milk traders, waiting in the wings, to break the milk cooperatives run by the milk producers themselves.

Such arguments, however, did not go down well with various impatient men. Finally, under the instigation of some milk traders, the men of those seventy-nine villages gave a call for a strike asking the milk producers not to give milk to their respective milk cooperative societies. In arriving at that decision they either had not consulted their wives or had told them very little about the proposed strike. The organisers at Dudhsagar acted promptly. They did not send back empty milk cans to those villages. Those cans, bearing the names of the striking villages, were piled up in the milk processing plant at Mehsana.

Since the women of those villages did not know much about the strike, they arrived at the milk cooperative as usual, waited in the queue, but were told later on that since their menfolk had threatened not to give milk to the cooperative, the dairy headquarters had neither sent the empty cans nor the trucks to carry them.

After that some families, desperately in need of money, sold milk to the traders at a vastly reduced price. Since milk is a perishable commodity, there was a panic to sell, and the people who benefited the most as a result of the call for a strike were those traders. Some families used the unsold milk for the purposes of making ghee (clarified butter). On the third day of the strike, irate women from several villages went to the secretaries of their respective village milk coops and asked them to get back those cans from the headquarters. Some of them even threatened to beat up the secretaries. Not only that, they themselves went to the dairy headquarters in Mehsana town, sat on its lawns as a gesture of protest, along with their children, and refused to leave until the organisers gave them a promise of the resumption of milk collection from their villages. Some of the women from the nearby villages even had their animals in tow as evidence of their willingness to sell the milk to the cooperative and to no one else.

In three days' time, the all-male milk strike fizzled out. Women claimed that since they were not involved in the decision for the strike, it was not binding on them. The men of the house shouted and screamed, and in some cases even battered their wives, but the women resumed their milk deliveries as usual.

The entire episode was an eye-opener for Dudhsagar. From then on they targeted women for all their development programmes in the district. It now came out with a fundamental shift in policy. Such a shift made the wife along with her husband a shareholder in the village milk cooperative society. Such joint membership, however, was given one vote. Nevertheless, such a provision gave women uninhibited access to the various decision-making meetings of the milk cooperatives. Soon after the institution of such a provision, all the villages in the district reported a phenomenal rise in women's attendance at various meetings.[1]

Moreover, the insurance on the life of the milch animal was now changed to the joint name of husband and wife, and so was the loan facility for purchasing milch animals, so as to ensure the joint ownership of the animal. And thus within a very short time women become the co-owners of the dairying resources of the family.

From the point of view of the organisers, the women were the pillars of the milk cooperative in the village. They believed that the women were more interested in the actual management of various activities relating to animal maintenance and milk production generally, and were therefore more likely to keep extraneous political considerations out of the day-to-day working of the organisation. This is because they looked at the organisation primarily as a means of family livelihood. But like everybody else, they too were competitive, and sought higher status for themselves through an added organisational position or advantage. But they were, nevertheless, more inclined to run the cooperative on a purely business-like fashion than did their menfolk. Apart from the usual squabbles and the excesses of over-zealousness, they did not want to use the institution of the milk cooperative, which was the means of their livelihood, as an instrument of political ambition, or to let anyone else use it in that fashion. In one instance, when the working of a milk cooperative in a village called Irana broke down as a result of in-fighting between two brothers and their factions, Dudhsagar, after a lapse of three years, restarted it in 1985. This time around it was turned into an all-women cooperative.

Moreover, as the organisers of Dudhsagar saw them, women were better team players in milk cooperatives than were men. They devoted all their energies to making the organisations a success once they got into them as women. Their entry there gave them a new identity and resolve. They felt that they were being watched by their communities and also by the top organisers at Mehsana. Under the circumstances they could not afford to fail. Consequently, they tried that much harder, and showed great willingness to listen and to enter into the process of give-and-take.

Dudhsagar's shift in policy, after the strike, opened up a great many possibilities for women. While they started attending meetings in increasingly bigger numbers, their own appreciation of the various provisions they could benefit from, as could be expected, took a great deal longer. Across the district their use of such provisions depended on initial help from liberal men or women voluntary workers working in the area. In those villages which provided such leadership, women were able to understand and benefit from such provisions. Elsewhere they had to wait till they developed adequate political capacity to be able to make use of them.

Let us now take into account the involvement of women in different sectors of the milk economy and identify the differentiated nature of their ascent wherever possible. We shall illustrate this by taking into account their involvement in five rural communities in the district of Mehsana.

Pamol

Among the milk-producing community in the district, the village of Pamol occupies the very top position. Its inhabitants are mostly Chaudhuries and their womenfolk have done a magnificant job of its milk industry by developing the famous *mehsani* buffalo to its ultimate productivity. For this they have earned the respect not only of the milk-producing community but also of the vets and animal traders. In 1987, Pamol, a village of six thousand, had an income of Rs.8.7 million (Rs.87 lakhs) from milk and Rs.5.7 million (Rs.57 lakhs) from its agricultural crops.

The Chaudhury women relate to their animals in a special manner. They tend to develop a deep and abiding interest in their animals. They tend to involve themselves by making the animal feel that it is a part of the family. They even use the human idiom to refer to them: "You see that buffalo over there, she is as old at my second son. Both were born within a few weeks of each other!" While there is an expressed feeling of gratitude among Chaudhury women towards the animal for having provided sustenance to the family, an extra income with which other things such as sugar, edible oil, vegetables, clothes, vessels, etc. were bought, there is also a tacit acknowledgement of the human bond with the animal.

Once the animals are tied in the family cowshed, the Chaudhury women are inclined to look at them as the intertwining of lives, human and animal, and from then on their feeling of togetherness grows. It is more than lives joined together by the Almighty to complete their respective earthly journeys. It is "them and us" together, right here in the present, sharing and sustaining each other.

The notion of sacredness as in the case of the indigenous cows was not there. Instead there was a complex range of notions of life, affection, bonding, togetherness, and a broader conception of family in which everybody's life, whether human or animal, was intricately mixed with everybody else's.

As a rule when a Chaudhury woman comes into the village, as a bride, she brings with herself a milch animal from her parents as part of her dowry. The dowry animal is referred to by means of an endearing term, *dhamani*. In the life of the young woman her *dhamani* buffalo, usually a *mehsani*, occupies a special place. It is a constant reminder to her of her parent's place. It therefore receives special attention. It is often singled out for a special scrub, pat on the back, display of affection, and an extra helping of cattle feed. Unlike other animals, *dhamani* buffalo, as a rule, die in the family cowshed. Schooled in looking after the *dhamani*, the Chaudhury women extend their training in maintaining their other animals. They even use a special term to express their feeling towards their animals. The term is *athwar*, indicating the human–animal bond.

Over the years, the Chaudhury women have developed their

own knack of understanding the moods of their animals. From the movements of the animal, and in particular from those of its skin, tail, eyes, ears, etc. they can understand the moods of an otherwise dull-looking animal. In return the animal recognises their voice and their directional commands.

The Chaudhury women have also acquired a deep understanding of the modern ways of improving the cattle breed and increasing milk productivity by means of cattle feed. Even the newly-introduced scientific techniques were suitably combined by them with whatever they, as the practitioners of animal breeding for generations, knew through their cumulative experience to produce results which always baffled the vets. With long experience, personal care, and modern science, they built the *mehsani* into one of the best milch animals of its kind.

Modern veterinary science threw yet another challenge at them in the late 1970s. That was in the shape of cross-bred cows. The local vets crossed and recrossed the indigenous cow with imported semen of Holstein–Friesian and produced a variety of high-yielding cross-bred cows which were known locally as the *shankar gai*. The milk yield of the *shankar gai* was roughly three times that of *mehsani*.

The economics of milk productivity convinced the Chaudhury males to make a switch to the new animal as soon as possible. For the Chaudhury women, however, the switch was not all that simple. To begin with there was something peculiar about the looks of the new beast. It was taller, humpless and graceless, with oversized udders, and, for the Chaudhury women, characterless. Since the *shankar gai* was a cow, its comparison with the local cows became inescapable. The local cow, and in particular the famed *kankarej*, originated from the neighbouring district of Banaskantha and, which had set the standard, had the most appealing look, with the beautiful curve of its horns, doe eyes, proportionate hump, and graceful movements of head and neck as she walked. Due to the lack of care in breeding over the years, its milk-giving span and capacity had dwindled considerably. And yet people who could afford such a majestic animal, for status and for all the right omens, went in for this near-barren but most beautiful animal. As opposed to that the *shankar gai* was just a plain and ugly beast with a single, and possibly decisive, virtue, namely productivity.

What was worse, the advent of the new animal was going to

take away from the Chaudhury women the role which they had gradually carved out for themselves. That role was one of breeding the animal to perfection, largely by means of human care, skill and kindness, and also scientifically-designed artificial insemination. But now such a role, with the introduction of the new animal was likely to be minimised. The vets and their cross-breeding records would determine the kind of animal combination, and frozen semen in nitrogen containers, would produce the higher- and higher-yielding animal. The new science, which came with the new animal of its own, diminished their role and responsibility as animal breeders. The Chaudhury women would now have much less to do, in a fundamental sense, with their animals. Their role as incomparable breeders had been usurped by the vets and stockmen leaving them with the sole function of milk extraction. Instead of an animal who had become a member of the family, what they were going to get, in their words, was a milk-vending machine in their cowshed.

The switch from the *mehsani* to the *shankar gai*, mercifully for the Chaudhury women, was neither swift nor complete. Neither the local vets nor the imported animal from other parts of the country could give rapid delivery of the new animal, with the result that most Chaudhury cowsheds had a mix of both animals. Despite the initial reluctance of the Chaudhury women to look at the new animal as their new ward, they were gradually getting reconciled to having them, and the local vets were confident that within a decade the Chaudhury women would do the same wonders, once again, that they did to the *mehsani*. They felt that despite the increased penetration of the veterinary science, no one can compete with the type of human care for the animal which the Chaudhury women were capable of.

Apart from the compelling economic consideration, the decision to switch from buffaloes to cross-bred cows was essentially a decision made by men. For they cultivated a greater sensitivity to the cost benefit of dairying than did their women. Moreover, their interaction with other men, who had a much wider range of exposure to information, and the collective sifting and digesting of such information in various gossip groups, persuaded them to be more exploratory, searching, adapting, and result-oriented. Even when the bits and pieces of male gossips were narrated to the women at home in the evenings, the latter's reaction often was "whatever you want to do, we shall do", and rarely "we do not want to do that". And in this particular instance, the women were double-minded, with more doubts than decisions coming out of them.

Men, in rural communities, were thus the effective source of new information, new example and new ways of doing things, and women, in the course of time, took on the operational responsibility of acting on them. Women too brought information through their own gossip groups, but before they were acted upon or reacted to, they wanted male corroboration of its certainty and validity. Such doubts were rarely expressed by women when men were the source of information.

In the end theirs were always family decisions in which men often played the initiating role, and the women one of initially doubting, half rejecting, and in the end of going along with it. But women were in most cases the implementers of decisions taken.

Most issues and problems on which decisions were required were common to one's cousins, kinsmen and neighbours. So the discussion on them was as much a family discussion as it was a discussion within the wider group, or a faction thereof, with which one socially interacted. The problem became one peculiar to certain families when they were either faced with a special kind of question, or with taking the initiative in introducing some new or different idea for the first time in the neighbourhood. In the context of dairying, however, the joining of the milk cooperative, the decision to administer artificial insemination, the decision to opt for a cross-bred cow, for all of these there were precedents.

Since the arrival of milk cooperatives in the district, a quarter of a century ago, the involvement of Chaudhury women had phenomenally expanded. The top organisers at Dudhsagar treated them not only as the principal units of their far-flung organisation, but even counted on their dedicated and disciplined way of working, experimenting, monitoring and, above all, standing by the organisation itself in the event of crisis. To the Dudhsager's veterinary staff they constituted an integral part of its own laboratory extending to different villages.

The ascent of Chaudhury women within the organisation of the dairy industry thus has been quiet and unceremonious without the usual claptrap of status. Most of them are themselves not aware of how important they have become to a modern, scientific, technologised organisation which has brought about significant economic changes within the district. And what is more, barring the tensions within certain families during the three-day milk strike, the ascent of the Chaudhury women in the economic and organisational matters of the dairy industry did not even pose the problem of family adjustment.

Gagret

The case of Chaudhury women, involved in the vortex of economic and social change brought about by milk cooperatives and also by the change in milch animals, was peculiar to them as women. Such a problem did not exist for the women of several other social groups.

In the village of Gagret, in the same district, a few miles away from Pamol, there was a high concentration of another agriculturist caste, namely the Patidars. Their women did not face the kind of problem the Chaudhury women, a close variant, faced. The Patidars, as stated earlier, concentrated more on agriculture than on dairying. They invested their surplus income in bore wells, and also in starting commercial ventures in the growing small towns such as Mehsana, Vijapur, Sidhpur, Harij and Patan, an old town. Such commercial ventures, and later on industrial ventures, were looked after by some members of the family, usually brothers or sons. So some of them always stayed behind in the village and looked after agriculture and dairying.

The Patidar women who looked after the family milch animals did not get deeply attached to the animal as did the Chaudhury women. For them the maintenance of milch animals was like cultivating land: they were as good as what you could get out of them. Such a businesslike approach made their shift to cross-bred cows a relatively painless exercise. The Gagret Patidars went for cross-bred cows in a big way and with great swiftness. For them it was a simple and attractive economic proposition. Their clarity of economic thinking, and swiftness in following it, had made them a relatively prosperous community in western India.

Ironically enough, the Patidar women, an integral part of a highly dynamic community, had a restricted economic role for themselves. For one thing not all of them accompanied their

husbands to their farms or worked with them for a part of the
day. For additional help, most Patidars, as a rule, employed
labourers on their farms. The Patidar women thus had a
minimum involvement in agriculture. The more the Patidar
prospered economically, the less they needed their women to
help them in their work on the farms. The Patidars even
developed a kind of reluctance, normally to be seen in upper
income groups, for working side by side with their women outside
the four walls of their houses. Similar constraints developed for
Patidar women so far as the looking after of the milch animal
was concerned. They did not go beyond the essential chores of
feeding, washing, and milking them. And when it came to taking
the animal to the village pond or taking the milk to the milk
cooperative, children were often asked to do that work.

Consequently, conventional notions of respectability, of what
the women of *ujadiat como* (upper caste groups usually consisting
of Brahmins, Banias and Patidars), can or cannot do, often
defined the parameters of work for Patidar women. Only the
educated Patidar women, those in urban centres, away from the
watchful eyes of the in-laws and neighbours, defied those
constraints.

Such a restriction of the area of economic activity also restricted
the scope of participation in various decision-making processes
for Patidar women. Insulated from such processes, Patidar
women were able to know less and less, or only as much as their
husbands had told them about events outside their four walls.

Within such closely related agriculturist castes as the Patidars
and the Chaudhuries, where traditionally accorded differences
were not so great, the different economic philosophies and what
was considered to be socially desirable or undesirable for their
respective womenfolk made all the difference, not only to women's
economic roles, but also to the extent of their participation in
public bodies, including their public expression of opinions on
wider issues.

But there was also another side to Patidar women. Despite
being a part of the rural community, the Patidar women were
also influenced by their own younger womenfolk who had
migrated with their husbands to the nearby town for commercial
and in some cases industrial, ventures. Those migrants set new
standards for household management, the education of children,
the marriage of daughters, travel, etc. which the rural Patidar

women admired and in some cases accepted for themselves. Such migrant Patidar women thus acted as a rural–urban link. But they, despite migration, had continued to leave economic decision-making, especially outside home, to their menfolk. In family matters, including the education of their children, their participation in decision-making came to have greater importance.

As the Patidars prospered, both in rural communities and in urban centres, the exclusion of their womenfolk from outdoor work and economic decision-making process continued more out of habit than as an act of deliberate exclusion. There again, there were many instances of their involvement in such a process especially in urban Patidar families.

As opposed to the Patidar women, the Chaudhury women remained co-partners in most of the economic undertakings of their men, and also in most decisions that were made about such undertakings. The Chaudhury economic prosperity did not progressively exclude women either as coworkers or as co-decision-makers. On the contrary, it involved them further in whatever new economic ventures their men got into.

Kakosi and Methan

Let us now briefly examine the two rural communities in the district which, apart from cooperative dairying, have become flourishing centres for selling and exporting milch animals to other areas of the country.

One of these is Kakosi. It is a large village of more than seven thousand people (1984). Its access road from the highway passes through a river bed. The relative inaccessibility of Kakosi by means of road has helped it maintain a distinct identity of its own. The population of Kakosi has a large proportion of Momens (Muslims). For centuries they have retained their Gujarati Muslim cultural identity and lifestyle. Its brightly-lit shops, a large number of restaurants, banks, schools and crowded streets give the impression that Kakosi is more of a town than a village.

For a long time Kakosi has been a centre of the milch animal trade. So very flourishing has been its trade that the former princely state of Baroda was persuaded to link it up with a railway line. It exports most of its milch animals to the city of Bombay. Bombay *tabelawallas* (cowshed owners) require a large number of milch animals. Consequently, Kakosi has flourished doing business with that metropolis. Kakosi collects its animals from within the radius of nearly one hundred miles. Apart from the railways, it also exports its animals by means of trucks, despite poor access roads.

Together with their trade in milch animals, the Momens of Kakosi also have a flourishing milk cooperative society. Like the Chaudhuries they too are considered to be very good breeders of animals. In that Momen women have played a very important role. But unlike the Chaudhury women, they do not get personally attached to their animals. They breed animals to export them and get the best value for their efforts. For them, for obvious reasons, the animal does not become a member of the family. They thus deliberately keep the human and animal kingdoms apart.

Such an approach is necessitated by the very nature of the milch animal trade in which their men are involved. These women have seen, day after day, some of the best animals loaded on the truck or train to Bombay. Then there is the return traffic of the near-dry animals from the Bombay *tabelas*. A returning animal is not a good sight to watch. Quite often it is difficult to revive their milk-giving capability. They are therefore sold at a low price or sent to the slaughterhouse. Apart from the animals kept for domestic and dairying use, the entire cycle of milch animal trade teaches Momen women to cultivate a professional distance and outlook on those animals.

As a rule the Momen women assist their men in selecting, pricing and loading milch animals on trucks and trains. But despite their equal involvement in the different stages of their trade, they have little or no say in decision-making. Their men tend to treat them as help in doing their business as they treat them in maintaining the household. Their judgement in assessing the animal's worth and pricing is also considered to be a form of household assistance which Muslim women are supposed to give, conventionally speaking, to their households. They thus neither have much say in domestic matters nor in matters of family business.

The other rural community which is also involved in milch animal trade is Methan, which almost adjoins Kakosi. Methan has a large population of Ismailis, who are followers of the Aga Khan. Like Kakosi it too has a flourishing milch animal trade with Bombay and an interest in the milk cooperative society. To both of these, the inhabitants of Methan bring a high degree of commercialism.

So far as their milch animal trade is concerned, they have an advantage over Kakosi. This is because the relatives of Methan inhabitants look after the Bombay end of their trade. Given such a link, animals are regularly brought back from Bombay for artificial insemination and another round of pregnancy, delivery and lactation. The cost of recycling the returned animal is often borne by the local milk cooperative as the traders are also shareholders in the local unit. Much to the annoyance of the district vets, this practice has continued over the years.

The Ismaili women of Methan are more educated than the Momen women of Kakosi. But like the Patidar women, despite their education, they too remain in the background so far as economic decision-making beyond the household is concerned. Methan women operate within the domain earmarked for them, conventionally speaking, by their men. But the Aga Khan, their spiritual leader, is very keen that women should take more education and get more extensively involved in their husband's activities, generally. Such an exhortation has resulted in recent years, in women getting more education and in helping their menfolk with account keeping in the family and in family business.

The Ismaili community in the village, as elsewhere, is a highly cohesive community. It also takes the *firmans* (advice-dictates) of the Aga Khan very seriously. Given their increasing level of education, and constant prodding by their spiritual leader, Ismaili women are likely to be more involved in decision-making processes in the years to come. The Aga Khan wants them to take to the professions of teaching, nursing, office-work, and other outdoor work. Such exhortations would therefore widen the area of economic involvement of Ismaili women and their participation in various decision-making bodies in the future. Their ascent, therefore, is much more a matter of how their men heed their spiritual leader and let their women come up in the future.

In 1987–8 Methan also constructed one of the largest biogas plants in the country. The impact of such a plant on the community is yet to be examined.

Borathwada

The village of Borathwada represents yet another situation for
the women of rural Mehsana. Its liberal leadership had made a
unique attempt at involving its women in all the structural
changes that were introduced for the purposes of development.
In order to develop the village by means of a series of cooperative
ventures, a number of new institutions were created. In each of
them women were given a high proportion of representation.
The moving spirit behind such an undertaking was a village
leader called Karsanbhai Chaudhury. He was a close associate
of Mansinhbhai Patel, the founder of the Dudhsagar milk
cooperative in the district. Both of them believed that unless
women came forward and worked in mixed male–female situations as equals, the rural community would not be able to
change the deeply-rooted notion of gender inequality. For that
purpose, therefore, a structural change based on gender equality,
involuntarily brought about in the beginning, would have a far-
reaching effect on succeeding generations. While Mansinhbhai
remained busy building a milk cooperative for the whole district,
Karsanbhai set a unique example, in the institutions of one rural
community, of restructured gender relationships.

Borathwada is located in one of the poorest regions of the
district. Its soil is sandy and its water saline. It is believed that
the area, in terms of geological changes, remained submerged
under sea water much longer than did the neighbouring land.

Such a natural limitation, however, had a positive side to it.
Since all in the community were equally affected by the poor
quality of the soil and water, all of them were willing to go along
with proposals which involved the entire community. Such a
background was a great help in launching ambitious cooperative
ventures, in different areas of the agricultural economy.

Then there was another reason for seeking a protective
cooperative shield. A few miles from the village, there was the
bustling town of Harij. It was dominated by the dynamic
commercial caste of Luhanas. The Luhanas of Harij had succeeded in developing commerce, banking, and educational facilities all of which had attracted a lot of development resources,
with the result that the rural communities within a radius of
fifty miles from it were left without such resources. Harij thus
represented an example of urban development at the cost of the
rural vicinity. One of the ways to fight such an unequal

development was through a cooperative organisation. Borathwada represented a unique example of such a struggle in the district.

In such a fight, Borathwada's internal social composition was not much help. Its population consisted of Chaudhuries (40 per cent), Thakardas (now known as Kshatriyas, 40 per cent), Rabaris (also known as Desai's, the traditional keepers of animals, 10 per cent), and then Venkars and other groups. None of these groups, not even the Chaudhuries of Borathwada were, economically speaking, in great shape. The village of Borathwada, within the Chaudhury social hierarchy, was way down. At the top of the hierarchy of that social group there were the Chaudhuries of those villages which had enjoyed the prestige of being a part of the revenue bureaucracy in the past. Then came the cluster of villages which came to be known as Bavisi (twenty-two) villages. Then there were groups of villages called Bora, Dator, Godhwada and finally, the Chovisi (24) villages. Borathwada belonged to the last group, Chovisi.

Such a low place within their own traditional hierarchy had another side to it. The Chaudhuries of Borathwada had much less hesitation in working with other lower castes. The question remains as to how long they would accept such a status, and look inside the village rather than try and introduce social distances between themselves and other lower castes so as to earn a good word from the Chaudhuries of other villages.

Borathwada's structural emphasis – of having cooperative institutions in various areas of the agricultural economy, and within them to have a fair representation for all the downtrodden castes and, above all, to provide a large representation to the women of all castes as a disadvantaged group – was the product of the social and political idealism of its own leadership. The inclusion of a large number of women in its newly-created cooperative institutions created problems of their own effective operation, especially of inspection at night, but the membership of women was not curtailed as a result. Borathwada also included a number of Harijan women who, till recently, were kept out of its institutions.

One of the most successful cooperative institutions which the village built was known as the Seva Society. It was designed to make use of government loans for buying farm implements, including tractors, and then renting them to shareholders for a small fee. It was founded in 1961.

Then in 1964, the village came to have the Khedut Piyat Society which owned and operated tube wells on a cooperative basis. In both these cooperative societies, there were women on the executive committees. Finally, the village came to have its milk cooperative society, when facilities for transporting the milk became available. Since women played an important role in the milk economy, a number of women were put on its executive committee.

Unlike the milk cooperative of Khadgodhara, a village which we shall examine later on, and which consisted entirely of women, Borathwada had a mixed composition. In Borathwada, women had no hesitation in working with men. Such an unmixed composition in Khadgodhara in fact had created difficulty for its women in graduating from an unmixed to a mixed situation.

In a sense the mixed gender composition of Borathwada was facilitated by its caste composition. The presence of certain higher castes often brings in the notions of respectability, expressed largely through gender distances and constraints. Their notions of status and female respectability, as we saw in the case of Gagret, tend to insulate their women from men, other than in the immediate family. The same is true of the Banias, upper-caste Rajputs and, of course, the Patidars. To such a rule Brahmins are often an exception. Since they are a traditional teacher-cum-leader caste, their women, as teachers and standard-bearers of certain new and desirable practices, are allowed to do a few bold things. Moreover, Brahmin respectability, earned by virtue of birth, is neither enhanced nor diminished by virtue of demonstrated conduct. Just that in matters of social conduct a Brahmin may feel called upon to set a standard.

So far as Borathwada was concerned, it had very few Brahmins and their women had agreed to work in the gender- as well as ethnic-mixed situations. Then there was a large number of Chaudhury women. Their inhibitions in working with men, and the objection of their men to let them do so was much less. And since Karsanbhai, the leading light of the village, was himself a Chaudhury, he saw to it that the Chaudhury women were not put to any disadvantage.

If there were inhibitions on women's part, they were largely confined to the middle-aged women. The older women, daughters of the village, or the widows among them were at ease with men. But during deliberations, the conventional seating distance between men and women, segregating men and women into two groups, with an occasional problem of *laaj*, had to be observed. So far as the bulk of younger women were concerned, they were busy with their household chores. However, when they did sit on committees, they showed a surprising ease in participating in the committee's deliberations. The most uninhibited women, in mixed situations, came from the Rabari community. Rabari women maintained that since the men of the village were like "uncles" or "cousins" to them, in kinship parallel terms, they had no hesitation in talking to them in the committees. And they were also the most vocal women, as vocal as they normally were in their family situations. Rabaris, a migratory caste, had neither institutionalised gender reticence nor distances. The same was also true of Harijan women. They too had much less hesitation in gender-mixed situations. However, their reticence appeared in ethnically-mixed situations. Since they always worked for others, often doing their menial jobs, they had deeply internalised their own notions of ethnic inferiority.

Within the various committees, the women did not experience a sense of conflict with men. On the contrary, most of them wanted men to give them direction. Moreover, the men–women relationship in various committees was seen by them through the perspective of the family. Families consist of men and women, so do committees. Within families men and women are related. Similarly, within committees they forge kinship parallel relationships to be able to relate to one another. And if there were differences of views and emphases, they were not different from similar differences in family, and were rarely on collective gender lines, and always on the lines of likes and dislikes of specific individuals.

Borathwada as a whole had put an enormous emphasis on education. The village had a number of well-known schools and some of their teachers had won national awards for their proficiency in teaching. It also had put a great emphasis on the education of women. And that is where it was a relative loser. While it educated and trained its girls, those girls, after marriage, went out to other villages. The girls who came into Borathwada as brides did not have the same educational standard. The question before it, therefore, was how to educate the incoming *vahus* (daughters-in-law). For this there were no simple answers. For one thing the *vahus* on arrival plunged themselves into their household chores and the bringing up of their family, at least in the first few years of their arrival.

The enormous emphasis on education in Borathwada, nevertheless, did help the *vahus* as well. Directly or indirectly they too picked up a little bit of education. Some through their school-going children, and others through specially-designed adult programmes for the busy *vahus*: Borathwada's educational prestige in the district was so high that the *vahus* who came into it expected to start, or resume their interrupted, education. In its various committees, the men and women of the village agonised over the question of how to bring the steady flow of the *vahus* into the village to its own standard of educational attainments, set for the daughters of the village.

The ascent of women in the foregoing five instances that we analysed was thus different in each case.

In the case of the Chaudhury women, the growth of the dairy industry in the district provided them with a great opportunity as breeders of milch animals to put to economic use the human skill of looking after the animals which they had developed for centuries. Those skills, instead of rivalling modern veterinary science, supplemented and blended with it. Even when the vets' visits to cowsheds increased, they depended more and more on the watchful care of the Chaudhury women to tell them how the new things, such as progeny testing, they had introduced were working. The arrival of the cross-bred cows had no doubt initially puzzled these veteran breeders. But it will be a mere matter of time before they decipher the latent codes of behaviour, of productivity, and of stimulus-response in general by which the new beast is governed. All in all, the economic importance of Chaudhury women grew as the dairy industry expanded in the district.

Simultaneously, along with other women, they also grew in organisational importance for the dairy industry in general. The complex network of dairy organisation in the district, with nearly a thousand village milk cooperatives, dealing with a highly perishable commodity such as milk, also involved in a life-or-death struggle against the wily and ruthless milk traders out to break the milk producers' organisation, together required a dedicated and loyal membership which would stand by it in fair weather or foul. The women of the district supplied to the organisation of Dudhsagar dairy such a stable foundation. Such recognition resulted in their induction as co-members, co-owners of their milch animals, and as co-decision-makers in its various bodies. In less than a decade, from the middle of the 1970s to the middle of the 1980s, women came to be recognised, formally, as the co-proprietors of the organisation of Dudhsagar itself, which is one of the largest in India.

The economic ascent of women in the district was thus a product of how they went about their work by means of their own traditionally-developed skills. As opposed to that their organisational ascent, because of the inherent social constraints in the traditional society, needed an extra hand from sympathetic men and humane institutions.

The Patidar women did not register a rise in importance so far as the economy of the district and its public decision-making bodies were concerned. They nevertheless did grow in importance through their rural–urban link of families. The segments of their extended families, which had migrated to towns, and even outside the country, were exposed to a number of the modernising forces of towns. Such segments, and especially the women in them, inevitably influenced those women who were left behind in the villages. Such a link gave to Patidar women in the villages a semi-urban outlook, style of dress, and style of life. Such an advantage was continually sustained by the urban link. Their ascent was therefore much more personal than economic.

The Momen and Momin women, despite their deep involvement in the economic activities of their husbands, did not register their own significant development in either personal or social terms. That was largely due to their sheltered, segregated, and rigidly defined area of activities. Potentially, in that respect, because of the constant prodding by their spiritual leader to educate women, the Momin Ismaili women had a greater chance of development. Together they represented instances of how orthodox men can cut down women's ascent by too narrowly defining the legitimate area of their activity.

Finally, the women of Borathwada who, because of the enlightened male leadership, were persuaded to participate in its various public institutions, registered significant gains both in public and personal terms. Despite being a backward rural community, its womenfolk, right down the social scale, not only participated in public bodies but also made significant contributions to their decisions. Such an advancement also led to their personal development through various social interactions and facilities. The ascent of women in Borathwada, in institutional terms, was the fruit of the efforts of its enlightened leadership rather than of the demands made by women themselves.

Taking all these instances together one finds that, barring the incident of the bulk of Chaudhury women disagreeing with their men going on strike, the ascent of women was facilitated by economic development, urbanisation and education, and institutional effort made by liberal-minded men. The rural women depended, far more than the urban, on some of those forces to help them rise in the scale of social importance. A good many studies on women in urban India, and also in Bangladesh, Pakistan, and Sri Lanka point to the same conclusion that women achieved substantial gains with men rather than against them or despite them.

SEGMENTED GENDER EQUATIONS AND SOCIAL INVOLVEMENTS

Officially speaking, nearly seven per cent of India's population consists of the Adivasis (tribals).[2] But within the Surat District of Gujarat, their population was close to half. Out of its thirteen sub-districts, nine of them were designated as tribal.[3] The tribals all along Indian history dodged and resisted the process of incorporation into Indian society as a whole. While such a resistance helped them to preserve their own cultural identity to different degrees in several parts of India, it has also put them outside the mainstream of economic and political development within the country.

To be able to help them catch up with what they historically missed, several institutional and public policy provisions have been made, particularly since Indian independence. This in turn has also created, to some extent, a self-serving elite within their ranks with only a few benefits trickling down to those among them who need them the most.

The main problem among them, as could be expected, is that of the mobilisation of the tribals in general so that they may learn to demand and utilise whatever has been earmarked for them. Towards such a mobilisation a variety of efforts have been made, some of which have been undertaken by bureaucrats, electioneering politicians, social workers, missionaries, and the vets from the milk cooperative of Sumul, which is located in the burgeoning city of Surat. Such agents of mobilisation have left behind their own imprints on the communities they tried to mobilise. Such imprints are also there in those communities where women have tried to participate. In this section we shall take up a number of such communities and identify the nature of their peculiar problems in operating public institutions or in participating in its decision-making policies.

Sumul Dairy in Surat District and its socially concerned vets got deeply involved in helping the tribals build village-level cooperative units. In 1984 Sumul claimed that close to two-thirds of its milk collection was from the tribal villages of the district. This was indeed a stunning achievement in rural development. Given the nature of tribal society, where the gender distance is much narrower, the vets did not have to make special efforts to involve women in the newly-created economic institutions.

The tribal villages, as a rule, have much less segmentation than do caste villages. Consequently, the tribal groups of the district such as the Chaudhuries (not to be confused with the Mehsana agriculturist caste), Gamits, Vasavas, Bhils, Senmas, Dhodias, Kotwalias, etc., while they do not intermarry, they nevertheless are much less set apart in their general social interaction than are the caste groups. As a result, an average tribal village, apart from its economic attraction, is far more amenable to cooperative activity than is a caste village.

Then there is also the difference between the claim to higher social status by certain groups and the traditional recognition of such a claim. Unlike caste societies not all segments in a tribal village concede the claims to ritual superiority of others. Barring the very low, the claim to such a superiority is neither aggressively pressed nor readily conceded.

Moreover, the claim to ritual superiority does not always prescribe a framework of constraints to women in tribal groups. Unlike caste groups, which use constraints on women as a mark of their cultural superiority, tribal groups do not single out their women for such a display of superiority. Consequently, problems which women face in tribal societies, particularly concerning their participation in the broader social and public life of their communities, are ones of the lack of familiarity with the operations of institutions, as in the case of their menfolk, rather than ones in which men have enjoyed special advantages. The traditional gender gap, or dominance–obedience role distinctions, that we find in a number of caste societies, are significantly absent in tribal societies. Such a gender equation provides an altogether different background to women's social involvements.

Let us now examine the specific instances of women's involvement in the social and institutional operations of a number of tribal societies.

The tribal village of Kadvali is situated about sixty miles from the city of Surat. Its main population consists of a tribal group called the Vasavas. Even by tribal standards, it is considered to be a backward village. Its soil is poor and it is entirely dependent on monsoon water.

In 1974, Jesuit missionaries arrived in the area and decided to adopt Kadvali as one of the villages for their activities. While they were primarily interested in spreading the Christian faith, they wanted to pursue it along with the economic development of the village. Consequently, along with their proselytising activity, they also emphasised education, provided medical aid, arranged classes for improving basket-making skills, and one of the missionaries went to the National Dairy Development Board, Anand, to take a course on how to organise a milk cooperative society.

The achievement of the missionaries in terms of the spread of the Christian faith was quite uncertain. That is because while a number of tribals "accepted" the new faith, they did not cease to believe in whatever they believed in before. The general polytheistic belief system of the tribals, the lack of any religious organisation to go with it, made them add, almost effortlessly, Jesus to their already-crowded pantheon of several gods. The missionaries insisted on the exclusivity of the acceptance of the Christian faith but that remained an unrealised wish. After nearly a decade of missionary activity, they confessed that they had hardly penetrated the outermost layer of tribal cultural system.

Culturally and socially, and in terms of gender relationships and role distinctions, Kadvali, despite missionary penetration, mobilisation, and institutional effort, did not change appreciably. One could see women at complete ease with men while working in the fields, in gossip groups, in smoking, drinking, singing or dancing parties, and within the institutions of the panchayat and the milk cooperative society. Whatever men could do or say, women could also do or say with effortless spontaneity. Round the circle of seated men and women, in an unsegregated situation, one could hear women talking and participating as much as men. Like men, women too took on the responsibility of measuring milk and keeping records in the milk cooperative. In their work they alternated with men without any fuss.

Kadvali was thus trying to develop itself, socially and economically, with equal participation by its women. In fact its antecedent gender equation had even helped it to accelerate the pace of its development by bringing in everyone's contribution towards a common social goal.

In most of the tribal villages, unlike in caste villages, no additional effort was required to associate women with local institutions. In other tribal villages called Ghata-Umerkuva in Surat district, with a mixed population of different tribal groups such as Gamits, Chaudhuries and Halpatis, no special effort was made to register women as members of the milk cooperative. And in 1984, out of its 300 shareholders, 108 were women, and only 13 among them were literate.

Their spontaneous response to membership of a public body such as the milk cooperative was indicative of the relatively little social distance between men and women in tribal villages. In such villages there was the unasserted, and unheeded, assumption that in most cases women can do what men can do. You did not have to educate, mobilise, exhort, or raise their consciousness to be able to bring home the point of gender equality.

Such a background did not create a problem for them when men and women found themselves in mixed situations. Even the competition for public office among them did not acquire a gender colouration or significance. There were pre-election dialogues in which no woman was told that a public office was not her cup of tea. Nor was there any shame in winning or losing against a woman. For all social and political purposes women were considered to be individuals like any other. Later on we shall see as to how the process of Hinduisation or *sanskritisation*, in the village, had reproduced the gender distance that one normally associates with caste villages.

Let us now examine the condition of women in a village which was considered to be, socially speaking, at the lowest rung of tribal hierarchy in the region.

As stated earlier, the claim to a hierarchical superiority among the Chaudhuries (tribals), Gamits, Vasavas, and Bhils, especially in Surat district, always remained unrecognised. To that extent the tribal society remained free from hierarchy as a desirable norm, which was at the heart of the traditional social organisation. However, when it came to the social standing of a group known as the Kothwalias, it was always referred to as the lowest of the low among the Adivasis. Some tribal groups even went to the extent of describing them as the "untouchables" among the Adivasis.

Among other things, the Kothwalias were the makers of baskets. But they could not always make a living out of it. Consequently, they used to go about scavenging for discarded food. That further reinforced the contempt of their fellow tribals towards them. Moreover, the Kothwalias were also considered to be the consumers of dead animals. It is said that skinners after detaching the skin of the dead animal would invite them to take away the meat of the dead animal.

Such a precarious living had often forced the Kothwalias to live on the edge of forests. Whenever they could not get food, they went into the forest and dug out certain kinds of roots and tubers, locally known as bhusaro and kano, and ate them. These were normally considered to be toxic. But the Kothwalias had special ways of processing them. And since they had been used to eating them since childhood, they had developed the necessary immunity to them. At the same time the protein value of those tubers was so great, it was said, that the Kothwalias after eating them could go without food for several days.

The eating habits of the Kothwalias, which they were forced to resort to from time to time, had thus brought down their status in the eyes of their fellow Adivasis.

One of their villages was called Kamlapur. During the British rule most of the cultivable land of the Kothwalias of Kamlapur had come into the hands of the rich Parsees from Bombay. Even its *gamtham* (residential area) which is normally considered to be unexpropriable, was taken away, reducing the village to a narrow strip of land along the highway. It will be difficult to find another village like Kamlapur which had very nearly disappeared. In

1977, government agencies and social workers bought back an area of fifty acres from the Parsees, and resettled them on it. The resettled portion was not contiguous with the strip of the surviving village by the roadside. The resettled village was also looked after by a social work organisation called the Manav Kalyan Trust. It helped the Kothwalias to rehabilitate themselves. It taught them new skills in basket-making, poultrying, fish farming, papad rolling, etc. All this was also done under the leadership of a Kothwalia woman. So then three agencies were involved: the Kothwalia woman, the social workers, and the trust. The Kothwalia woman was the critical link between the social workers and the trust and her own people. She was the communicating link. While every Kothwalia appeared to respond to the suggestions and advice of the bureaucrats in the office of the trust, on crucial matters the community of Kothwalias waited for the decision from the woman.

The Kothwalia woman was the chairman of the milk cooperative, and also of the local council. In all the economic undertakings of Kothwalias, managed by the trust, the average person was both a wage-earner and shareholder. The trust also helped them to organise a milk cooperative society which was connected with Sumul. Furthermore, the trust had arranged for a diamond polishing unit in the village and young Kothwalia males were given training for it. Diamond polishing had become a very lucrative industry in the district. Boys between the ages of 14 to 18, after training could earn as much as Rs.800 to Rs.1200 per month.

While economically Kamlapur had seen better days in the mid 1980s, no one was willing to bet on its continued economic prosperity, given the record of the Kothwalias in the past. The woman whose leadership turned around the fortunes of Kamlapur never for a moment faced questions concerning her actual or potential capability. Strangely enough the questions concerning female adequacy, in her leadership role, came only in villages with upper-caste composition, or in what was considered to be relatively "advanced" villages. The men in those villages even conspired to bring down women from positions of power by means of character assassinations and jibes for their being "women" and therefore brainless or ignoramuses or soft. For such men the mark of their superiority, and macho claims, had to be accompanied with their underlying assumption that they, the men, exceeded women in political skill and management. They invariably said, *"rajniti ae bairanu kam nathi"* (politics are not for women). This remained their unexamined and unshakable premise, from which they derived many inferences and judgements. Ironically enough, Kamlapur, the village of the most socially-backward people in the region, had established the most stunning example of women's leadership and gender equation.

At the other extreme there were those tribal communities which had started imitating the ways of caste or "advanced" villages, and with such a process also came the gender distances that were implicit in them. One of them is Khuntadia which is situated about ten miles from a small town called Vyara in Surat district. In the pre-independence days, Khuntadia was a part of the former princely state of Baroda which had put enormous emphasis on the education of boys and girls. In the early 1980s some of the Adivasi girls from the village had even graduated with degrees from the nearby town of Vyara.

Khuntadia was largely populated by the tribal groups known as Gamits. Gamits are considered to be more advanced than their fellow tribals. Through its education and proximity to the town of Vyara, Khuntadia had not only acquired a number of urban influences, and was therefore rapidly losing its cultural purity, or whatever was left of it, but it was also trying to "sanskritise" some of its ritual practices. Under the circumstances one could notice a lot of Hindu ritual observances along with Indian film songs, dances, and dresses in place of the tribal ones. It was not clear at that stage how the notion of hierarchy would transpose itself, in the process of emulation, within the social structure of the Gamits, the predominant tribal component of the village.

But what was most significant was the behaviour of the Gamit women. They were partly segregated from men, and some of them even observed the *laaj* by lowering their *odhanis* (tribal equivalent of sarees) in the presence of men from the village. The assimilation of such segregational norms had also affected the participation of women in public life. While it was common for any relatively backward tribal village to have women participating spontaneously with men in mixed situations within public institutions, the semi-urbanised and "sanskritised" Gamit women of Khuntadia had observed the self-imposed social distance between themselves and their menfolk. And within such a social distance there was also the tacit acceptance of certain rigidly-defined gender domains. Khuntadia had thus inadvertantly imported gender inequalities. The price which the Gamit women paid for their social "progress" was extracted in terms of a more stringent re-arrangement of what they could or could not do as women.

Gamit women of the older generation, it was heartening to notice, had not internalised the new norms of gender distance. They were therefore much less inclined to be treated as unequals. Unlike the women of the middle and younger generation, the Gamit women of the older generation moved around spontaneously with men, spoke and raised their voices at them as they chose, and gave the impression of an unsurrendered equality. That was in marked contrast with their "forward" daughters and daughters-in-law, whose participatory voices were increasingly smothered by the new norms of what could or could not be said in mixed company.

LEARNING TO FACE A VARIETY OF OPERATIONAL PROBLEMS

In some of the villages of Surat district, men used women in positions of authority to defraud public institutions of their money. The milk cooperatives of Sumul reported three such cases. In each of them women in charge of milk cooperatives depended on their husbands for help and, in particular, the management of cash. The proximity to cash proved far too tempting to the latter. In those three cases an Anavil Brahmin women (Dindoli), Muslim women (Gholvad), and a Patidar woman (Delwada), respectively, were unable to check the misdeeds of the men who were supposed to help them. In that connection the case of Dindoli was important because it did have a harmful effect on the livelihood of the economically depressed group called the Halpatis. Let us therefore examine it in some detail.

Situated on the outskirts of the city of Surat, Dindoli was selected as a pioneer in women's milk cooperatives in the district. Unlike other tribal villages of the district, Dindoli had an ethnically-mixed composition with a large population of Halpatis.

Dindoli had an active women's organisation consisting of housewives and school teachers from the upper castes. They spearheaded the idea of a women's milk cooperative. Sumul Dairy on its part put the condition that they include Halpati women as shareholders. That was acceptable to the upper-caste women. When the village milk cooperative was organised, a dedicated Anavil Brahmin woman, who was a schoolteacher, became its chairperson.

During the first two years, the women's milk cooperative worked very well. It was able to enrol a large number of Halpati women as shareholders, and to help them obtain loans for buying milch animals, and thereby increase their income.

While the Halpati women looked at the new economic institution with a lot of hope and loyalty, a number of upper-caste women on its executive committee treated it as a means to power, status, and as a springboard for a role in district or state politics. Such women became increasingly unresponsive to the demands of the shareholders.

In the course of time the initial warmth and collective aspiration for achieving something unique gave way to minimal courtesies. The enforced social equality within the organisation, between the women of the upper castes and Halpatis, was gradually eroding. The Halpati women wanted to know more about the working of the organisation and each time they tried they were rebuffed. On their part, psychologically and politically, the Halpati women, despite their sizeable number, were unable to press their demands to know more about the working of the organisation. Their suspicions were further aroused because they were given different figures at different times by way of the balance of their loans.

In the meantime the audit department of Sumul discovered a lot of irregularities in the accounts of the Dindoli milk cooperative. While the shareholders, and in particular the Halpati women, were regularly paying off their loan instalments, those amounts did not always reach the bank which had loaned them the money. Moreover, the money which was supposed to go to them by way of bonuses, etc. at the end of the year, was also not paid. Finding the financial irregularities too grave, Sumul reluctantly decided to close down the milk coop rather than take the embezzlers to the court.[4]

In this entire episode the Halpatis were given a raw deal. Since the upper-caste women were used to treating them as domestic servants, they were not quite reconciled to being accountable to, of all people, the Halpatis. Even when the latter sat in the public office, they were viewed from the point of view of their former or current economic relationship with the women of the upper caste. Moreover, on their part, the Halpati women had deeply internalised a notion of their own inferiority as a result of their unequal economic status. Consequently, even when a Halpati woman saw some economic impropriety committed by an upper-caste woman, she could not muster sufficient courage to question and check it publicly.

It is interesting to note here that social inequality among women in the milk cooperatives of other villages was much less a barrier than it was in Dindoli. In other milk cooperatives, with unmixed situations especially, women seem to be less aware of their social distances. And if the women of the upper caste came ahead of other women in leadership roles in such situations, it was perceived as a part of the cultural and educational advantages which they had otherwise enjoyed. Once in such a role, the women of the upper castes identified with their gender group, i.e. women, rather than carry forward their traditional caste advantages to reflect divisions within society. In that respect the case of Dindoli was the other way round. The upper-caste women in it had carried forward their class superiority into their gender group. Politically they wanted the support of their gender group for local as well as district and state politics. But in return they were not willing to pay the smallest price which an ambitious politician in democratic India, with a hierarchical social organisation, has to pay, namely electoral lip service to the ideals of social equality.

The search for narrowing the gender gap, the Dindoli example points out to us, is only one of the many gaps to be narrowed. Since the gender gap is one of the most visible of gaps, we seem to turn our attention to it more often. But what is alarming is that in the very effort at narrowing it we may bring in, or reinforce, some other inequalities.

There were also many instances where women in either mixed

situations, or situations totally dominated by men, had occupied statutory positions and had done a commendable job of what they were entrusted with. In some cases their work was so good that formal resolutions were passed commending their work. In most cases such work was of a sustained quality spread over a few years. The milk cooperative in a village called Butanwada, which is a Patidar dominated village, was almost entirely composed of men so far as its decision-making bodies were concerned. The lone exception to this was a Patidar woman who acted as its secretary.

The membership of the village was so grateful to her, for her dedication and efficiency, that it had even placed on record its appreciation by means of a formal resolution. Then there were three tribal villages, the institutions of which had men as well as women in their decision-making bodies. They were Ghoda, Tokarwa, and Waghnera. In each of them tribal women played an important part as their secretaries in milk cooperatives. Then there is the village of Kathor, which is on the outskirts of the sprawling city of Surat. The milk cooperative there consisted of a number of economically backward social groups including Halpatis, Harijans, Vasavas, Gamits, etc. Its chairwoman was a woman from the Dhobi (washerman) community and its secretary was a Muslim woman. Together they had made the milk cooperative into an exemplary body. Finally there was the example of lower-caste and tribal women working together, in the villages of Golan and Valod in the Lizzat Papad Cooperative under the supervision of men who subscribed to Gandhian ideology. This cooperative is a great success and a lot of scholars have written on it.[5]

Before we leave this short section, it might be of interest to note that women as organisers, *vis-à-vis* men and *vis-à-vis* other women, face some peculiar problems. They are problems relating to their initial years of public participation in a domain which was, until recently, a preserve of men.

The organisers at Sumul headquarters repeatedly mentioned that women in charge of public institutions often take far too long to take decisions on crucial issues. They seem to seek advice from too many diverse sources which often confuse them. Their fears of taking wrong decisions are vastly exaggerated by themselves. They therefore give the impression of being weak and vacillating. Quite often the organisers at Sumul had to "extract" decisions from them with the assurance that they, the women, would not be held responsible for them.

Then it was also pointed out that the present generation of women in rural communities have genuine difficulty in grasping the intricacies of accounting systems. Women, despite some training, often showed aversion to, or fear of, accounting. Consequently, they often brought in men to do that work for them. Such an approach did not always work to their advantage. As we had seen earlier, such men often got women into difficulty by being either careless or just plain greedy for others' money. In practically all the instances where women financially defaulted, the real culprits were men who were entrusted with the cash or accounting or both.

Women also showed much less confidence in other women. They seemed to trust men much more. This was because they had deeply internalised what men had told them for ages, and that is that women were inferior to men. Consequently, when a woman did well, she often felt that she, alone, had now entered man's world, and that other women were not as smart as herself. In adopting such an attitude, women in authority were often unduly unkind to other women and often needlessly antagonised them.

There was a parallel between a successful woman's attitude to other women and a colonial situation. Within the colonial situation you are persuaded to develop vertical loyalties. That people above you are superior and are worth being with. People at par are not worth your while. So then a successful woman preferred to be with men in office like herself rather than be a channel of communication, and a conduit, for a lot of change that was needed to help other women.

Then there was the problem of women getting hooked on a new programme. Often the same group of women came forward for all the newly-introduced rural schemes. They grabbed all the fresh opportunities, and once they entered the establishment, they looked upon the similar progress of others unfavourably. Some of those women, like men, were also becoming subsidy or largesse-minded. They were continually looking for help from outside.

Finally, in this line of argument, the present generation of women in rural areas, with the exception of tribal women, had a real problem of working in mixed situations. Within the unfamiliar mixed situations, women often had problems of excessive self-awareness and the anxiety of making fools of themselves in front of others. Consequently, they either were speechless or flustered, and would often end up taking positions, or acting in a manner, they normally would not. Barring the tribal women, those at home in mixed situations were the older women from the upper castes and possibly widows.

These, however, were problems faced by a society in transition, moving from an exclusively male-dominated social situation to one where women were slowly making an entry into public institutions, and altering the attitude of men towards them, and in that process themselves learning to live and act in mixed situations.

THE BITTER TASTE OF GRADUATING FROM UNMIXED TO MIXED SITUATIONS

Khadgodhara, a village in Kaira District, represents one of the earliest attempt to involve women, institutionally, in the management of the milk economy. The village has a mixed population of Patidars, Kshatriyas, Muslims, Venkars, etc. For a long time it was considered to be a village of outlaws, and therefore one which administrators consistently avoided visiting. Even for the establishment of a milk cooperative in the area, the preference, in the beginning, was for a neighbouring village and not for Khadgodhara.

The dislike of the administrators and the indifference of the Amul dairy organisers towards Khadgodhara began to change from the middle of the 1960s onwards as a result of the dynamic leadership of a Brahmin widow. She and her husband had raised their family in the nearby town of Kapadwanj. But after the children had grown up, and when her husband passed away, she returned to Khadgodhara, which was her husband's village. Soon after that she involved herself in social work in the village. The villagers were so very impressed with her work and dedication that they elected her to the *panchayat* (local council), and later on as its *surpanch* (chairperson). Being an elderly lady, a widow, and also an educated Brahmin with a lot of confidence in herself, she had no hesitation in working with men.

Her next target was the establishment of the milk cooperative

society in the village itself. Already there was one in the
neighbouring village which was about a mile from Khadgodhara.
But that was not convenient to women, particularly in the
evenings during the monsoon and winter. Moreover, the large
population of Muslims in the village did not approve of their
women going out to another village.

She therefore approached the top organisers of Amul dairy in
Anand and tried to persuade them to let her have another milk
cooperative in her own village. For that the top management
put one condition, and that was that the Khadgodhara milk
cooperative should be virtually constituted and run by the
women themselves.[6]

Such an institutional provision, although initially fraught with
the danger of not getting off the ground, admirably suited the
Brahmin woman, and to her own surprise the women of the
village, and in particular those from the Muslim community,
were most enthusiastic. In the shortest possible time, therefore,
she was able to enrol a large number of women as its shareholders.
Then a managing committee entirely consisting of women had
to be elected and so did its chairwoman. That too proved to be
very simple, the committee naturally elected the Brahmin woman
who had spearheaded the idea.

Since the women of the village now had an institution of their
own, with an unmixed composition, they relegated the work of
the *panchayat* to men. For quite some time the milk cooperative
and the *panchayat* worked admirably within their separate
domains. The trouble began when women with experience of
the democratic process, in the unmixed situation of the milk
cooperative society, had nowhere else to go but to the village
panchayat with its mixed composition. For a while they hesitated
and kept themselves in a political limbo. Finally, when they
gathered sufficient courage to involve themselves in the fiercely
competitive democratic politics of the *panchayat*, not only did
they experience a lot of problems, but the hostile repercussions
of such an involvement were felt even inside the milk cooperative
society itself. This was largely due to certain families having
their respective men and women in these two public bodies.

Let us now examine the problem of transition from unmixed
to mixed situation in some detail. Khadgodhara presented a
unique instance of inducting women, across the ethnic divide,
into the democratic process. Their initial induction in such a

process took place within the secure walls of the unmixed situation of the milk cooperative where everyone from the shareholders to the chairperson were women. Such a provision suited their menfolk who wanted their women to stay away from other men.

But that was true only up to a point. For even within the unmixed milk cooperative, women were not totally insulated from men. The coop women, as a matter of routine, came in contact with vets, the coop secretary, stockmen, dairy officials from Amul, etc. who were all men. Such an operative reality of mixed situations, which, however, did not go unnoticed by men, was resented the least. Consequently, the baptism of women into public life, through the milk cooperative, which was avowedly unmixed, was in actual practice very different. It prepared them, as it were, for the next stage of their political ambition, if they had any.

In their gradual political emboldenment, however, what also mattered a great deal was their own ethnic background, age, marital status, and last, but not least, the attitude of their menfolk.

The elderly Brahmin women, as we saw earlier, moved with ease from a mixed to an unmixed situation and back again to the mixed. The next in line for such a movement was a Brahmabhatt woman, of middle age, who was a deputy to the Brahmin woman in the milk cooperative. She too moved from the unmixed milk cooperative to the mixed *panchayat*, along with the Brahmin woman, but not without certain adverse political repercussions for herself.

But such a shift from unmixed to mixed situations for Kshatriya, Venkar (ex-untouchable), and Muslim women, who had also graduated from coop politics, was, for a variety of reasons, unthinkable at the current stage of Khadgodhara's social and political development. For one thing their menfolk did not want their women, who were relatively far more sheltered than Brahmin and Brahmabhatt women, to go out into the mixed situation of the *panchayat* and rub shoulders, as it were, with men there. The milk cooperative in the village, which was entirely managed by women, was in the mid 1980s nearly two decades old. But that had not broadened the male horizons. And on their part the women depended, as always, on the approval and moral support of their men, despite their experience of the milk cooperative, before they could plunge themselves into *panchayat* politics. In fact these women repeatedly complained that their men would not like them to go beyond the unmixed milk cooperative. In their cases, therefore, men still continued to define the extent of female political territory.

In a sense the women of Khadgodhara, who were schooled in the democratic politics of the milk cooperative, were ready, or at least the active among them were, to try their hand at *panchayat* politics. This is because they too had experienced electoral contests in running their institutions. But there was also a basic difference. Since the milk cooperative was a source of supplementary income, and a means of livelihood, the electoral contestants within it often refrained from carrying their grudges too far. Moreover, all along they were made to feel that they were being watched by the whole village, the district, and above all the dairy officials at Amul. Such an awareness often made them feel that they had to give a good account of themselves as women. Every time they had to prove that the predictors of their failure were wrong. So after each electoral strife, there was much greater effort at accommodation and the need to work together. Such a preparation in democratic politics would have been ideal for *panchayat* politics, but the events in the village somehow did not shape that way.

The milk cooperative society also created problems for politically ambitious women by forcing them to move on to other public institutions after a spell in it. Since there was an understanding, right from the start, of the rotation of office for women, after every two to three years, the question of what to do with the coop retirees was not clearly thought through. The alternative, at the time of formulating the rotation principle was couched in the vague, and even idealistic, language of "everyone must get a chance to serve the community".

The milk cooperative for women, by and large, was the handiwork of the Brahmin woman. Until recently she was the moving spirit behind the organisation. Consequently, between her and her colleagues there was initially a lot of difference in leadership skill and political experience. Moreover, her colleagues, who later on emerged as equally good in political skill, continued to treat the Brahmin woman, for some time, as the maîtresse at whose feet they sat and learnt all about democratic politics. The political hold of the maîtresse on her protégés

continued during the initial years of her rotation-enforced
retirement. Her women political trainees listened to her for some
time, especially on the question of who should succeed who by
way of rotation for the office. This resulted in a couple of smooth
successions, a Kshatriya woman followed her, and then she was
followed by a Brahmabhatt. Both of them were her creations
and in a sense the maitresse began playing the role of a succession
selector or a queen-maker. Then came the turn of a Venkar
woman (ex-untouchable), and a Muslim woman. In both the
cases what tipped the electoral balance was the numerical
following of these two social groups among the shareholders of
the milk cooperative. The unusual comments that these two
women did not have education or experience, which were
euphemisms for social prejudice, did not go very far in the coop
election of 1986. With the failure of all the political machinations
also ended the effective role of the maîtresse as the queen-maker.
All institution builders in a democratic process have to surrender,
sooner or later, their advantaged access to political power, no
matter how much they get attached to it.

Politically, the only avenue left for the milk coop retirees was
the *panchayat* itself. From the point of view of the coop retirees,
they had graduated in public work from the milk coop and were
now ready to serve, through the *panchayat*, the wider community.
Such a logic, however, did not sit well with the members of the
panchayat who were mostly men. From their point of view, they
had already agreed to create a separate body for women and
that was the milk cooperative, and the women, they hoped would
respect the gender divide between the two institutions. The only
place for women in the *panchayat*, according to them, were the
two seats reserved for women by law. From their point of view,
therefore, women should neither ask for nor get more seats in
the *panchayat*. Men kept out of the milk coop, and now women
should keep out of the *panchayat*. They should not contest general
seats and least of all the chairmanship of the *panchayat* itself. To
let them have the *panchayat* as well would be tantamount to a
gender monopoly.

The two women retirees from the milk coop did not accept
such an argument. One of them was, naturally, the Brahmin
woman, and the other one was the Brahmabhatt woman, her
protégé, and also another milk coop veteran. Both of them
contested elections for the general seats, defeated their main

rivals, and became chairperson and deputy chairperson, respectively, of the *panchayat*. The men felt disgraced and the intensity of their humiliation, as could be expected, was going to complicate further the politics of the village.

But in her political fight against men, the Brahmabhatt woman, in particular, was most vulnerable. This is because she was also an employee of the milk coop as a health worker. In that capacity she had done remarkable work in the early detection of a large number of tuberculosis cases and other illnesses in the village. Consequently, the health officers at the Tribhuvandas Foundation in Anand were full of praise for her.

The men who had lost their *panchayat* elections against the two women persuaded the women in the milk coop to stop the salary of the Brahmabhatt woman and suspend her from work. The coop was not supposed to take such an action on its own. It had thus transgressed the limits of dos and don'ts imposed on it by the Foundation in Anand. The Foundation, being in an unforgiving mood, closed down the health unit in the village. It promised to reopen it only when the village sorted out its own politics and not let it spill over the vital area of health care.

The women of Khadgodhara were thus forced to learn their own political lessons in electoral strife and post-electoral accommodations. They were also forced to realise that in order to survive in politics, either in the coop or in the *panchayat*, they would have to develop the commensurate political skill for effective results and, from time to time, reach accommodations for their own political survival.

So far women with education did not feel obliged to participate in the political life of the village. In the winter of 1984, the village reported that as many as twenty-five girls attended a degree college in the nearby town. Ten of these girls, because of the facilities provided by missionary institutions, were from Venkar families. Those girls, however, did not have much interest in village public life. Since they, as a rule, were going to be married outside the village, their impending departure did not stimulate their interest in the problems of the village.

At the other extreme, educated girls who were married into Khadgodhara, took time to raise their family, cultivate a taste for public life, and then persuade their menfolk to allow them to participate in it. Towards that a background was already prepared by the women who involved themselves in the running of the milk coop as well as the *panchayat*. Now it was for the next generation of women to extend that area of their involvement in public life and not get demoralised by the rough and tumble of politics which involved men and women in mixed situations.

RELUCTANT PARTNERS IN SEASONAL MIGRATION

This then brings us to an examination of the migrations of the tribals of Panchmahal District and the Maldharis or Bharwads of Surat District, and the unwillingness of their women, in particular, to continue their age-old pattern of migration. The tribals, as stated earlier, in order to avoid assimilation in the wider social organisation, and historically also to dodge the wrath of the conquerors, had withdrawn themselves into the hilly terrain or forests of India. Consequently, economically their means of survival and development in general had been far more limited than those of other social groups.

Among the tribals, some of the poorest of the poor are to be found in the hilly regions of Panchmahal District in western India. They are able to get not more than one crop during or soon after the monsoon every year. That too of poor quality. Consequently, unlike the tribals in other parts of the country, including Surat District, those from a number of villages in Panchmahal District are forced to go in search of work as labourers in towns where there is substantial house-building or road-construction activity. Every year they migrate to such places for a period of six months, from October to March. The remaining six months in a year they spend in the villages looking after their monsoon-based single crop.

Their migration for work often follows a set pattern of season, place, nature of work, and even wages. Those among them, for instance, who go to towns such as Ahmedabad, Baroda and Anand, where there is a lot of building activity year after year, keep going to the same place, do the same kind of work, usually for the same building contractors, and get wages with little or no increase. They seasonally migrate from their villages in Panchmahals in groups along with their women, children, a few belongings and the usual means of transport of goods, namely mules. They almost always travel by road in groups of fifty to two hundred and then distribute themselves in various parts of the towns where building activity is going on. Since they have neither a good sense of the going rate of wages for non migrants in the town nor enough skill in putting collective pressure on the building contractors, they often end up by having a raw deal at the hands of their employers. Moreover, most of them start negotiating after their arrival on the spot when it is often too late to threaten the employers with alternative job possibilities. Consequently, season after season, they return to their villages with little or no savings.

Various rural development agencies have realised that there is a basic economic reason behind such a migration and unless an additional source of income is found for them, they will not be able to stop such a migration which is almost always so very unsettling to their families. Consequently, a number of attempts are now being made to help them to stay in the village, possibly get better returns from their fields, and supplement it with an income from dairying. For this purpose better seeds, fertilisers, and improved water facilities are now being increasingly provided to them. But such a provision so far has been far from adequate.

Then there is the attempt made to give them a subsidy for buying milch animals. There again the results are uneven. Some villages have done exceedingly well whereas others have treated the subsidy as a means of buying a milch animal and then disposing of it at the first available opportunity. Moreover, the sudden arrival of a milch animal, with the need to look after it all the year round, has created problems for those families which have been used to seasonal migrations. Such families often hand over their newly-acquired milch animals to their relatives or neighbours and continue to do the usual round of migration. In their absence, their animals do not get the care and attention that they normally need and thereby their milk-giving capacity gets increasingly diminished.

The migratory families are not without their own conflicts. Those that stay behind in the villages gradually improve their fields, get good returns from their milch animals, and, if necessary, do for a short while *majoori* (unskilled work) on nearby road-building sites but stay on their farms. Such tribals also make fun of those who are gone for too long from their fields and animals in order to make a living in the cities.

Moti Jari, a tribal village about twenty miles from the town of Godhara, from where a number of families used to migrate seasonally, saw a gradual decline in such movements. Instead most of its inhabitants took to dairying and did a splendid job of it. The district milk cooperative, Panchmahal Dairy, reported a phenomenal rise in its milk collection all the year round from the village, with a relatively very high fat content. Even the village post office indicated an increase in savings accounts and the amount of money deposited since the establishment of the milk cooperative in the village.

The non-migrant residents of Moti Jari, as stated earlier, often made fun of those who continued with their migratory habits. Each one of them was a veteran of such an experience. And he or she had horror stories to tell as to what happened to them while working for contractors in the towns, and how very little were they able to save after six months of hard work, far away from their homes, relatives and friends. Those who continued to migrate from among them were on the defensive. None of them was able to say that he saved much more than he would have been able to do had he decided to stay in the village.

The women among such migratory groups were often more unwilling to continue their annual rounds to the towns to do hard work there, to live in makeshift huts, and to return to the village only to be told that their trip had hardly benefited them financially. But year after year they also succumbed to the persuasions of their males. They, nevertheless, were finally responsible for discouraging their families and neighbours from continuing their migratory rounds. But that did not diminish the volume of such migrations. While some families dropped out, others joined in, year after year.

The improvement in agriculture and dairying as sources of supplementary income, was slow to come by. In the meanwhile what actually helped the women to tip the balance in favour of non-migration was the possibility of finding work on a road construction site, or of reforestation under the programme of what is known as Social Forestry. It was considered to be an answer to India's dwindling forests. Under this programme, eucalyptus and subabul (a local variety of tree) seeds were grown in nurseries at a distance of ten to twelve miles on the roadside. Then between October and May, rows of holes were dug on the two sides of the roads, railways, canals, farms, factories and offices. Soon after the first rain, the seedlings were planted for the monsoon of June to September to take care of their early growth. The success rate in such a scheme of planting, it was reported, was more than 80 per cent.

If work of that, or a similar nature, in particular road repair, in the neighbourhood was available during the period of transition from a migratory to non-migratory pattern of life, then some of those tribal communities came out of the highly unsettling and economically unrewarding migratory cycle.

The availability of that kind of work helped women and the families in general to decide what to do. Such decisions were made by a group of neighbourhood women, along with men, amidst a lot of screaming and arguments and vagueness as to what was finally decided. Such decisions are not women versus men decisions. They are essentially family and group decisions where the voice of women is more effective. That is because women are not merely central to the annual migratory enterprise, but also the principal organisers of such movements. Men rarely travel by themselves. With women come children, belongings and mules, all in one package. Migrations, then, are of families and not of individuals, and the women play an organising role in it. Consequently, the pattern of seasonal migration, apart from its economic attraction, continues as long as women support it.

Let us now examine yet another instance of women taking a lead in discouraging seasonal migrations. In Surat District an extraordinary episode of the Bharwad caste – the traditional keepers of animals and a migratory people for centuries – was reported. They gave up their migratory movements and settled in a village. In reaching that decision their women had played an important part.

The Bharwads describe themselves, of late, as Maldharis. Mal is a term used to refer to livestock. The term here therefore referred to the owners of livestock. They came increasingly in conflict with farmers who resented their traditional occupation of grazing their animals on the outskirts of fields and sometimes letting the animals stray into fields with crops. While the male Maldharis were used to arguments and fights defending their traditional right to graze their animals on the non-private land, their womenfolk were getting tired of it. Moreover, the Maldhari women had also noticed, enviously, women of various villages building their own lives round their settled way of life, sending their children to schools, and in most cases displaying some economic progress. Maldhari women too now wanted such a lifestyle for themselves and their families. They wanted their children to have education which the children of other families had. They therefore persuaded their husbands to explore the possibility of a settled living. The men concurred and spoke about it to the officials of the Sumul dairy. The officials of Sumul, on their part, persuaded the residents of a newly-separated village called Uchhvan. Uchhvan was formerly a part of Umarpada. While the Umarpada shopkeepers wanted the Maldharis to settle in their village, in the interest of their own business, some of the farmers did not. In the meanwhile when a new village was carved out, separating Umarpada from Uchhvan, the officials of the new village let them settle in one locality of it provided they pursued their traditional occupation of animal breeding as settled people and not as a migratory community taking their animals from the outskirts of one field to another.

The Maldharis of Uchhvan thus broke their traditional migratory cycle of centuries. Since their non-migratory life started only recently, in 1979, it remains to be seen how they actually fare. In the 1983 and 1984 interviews of Maldhari women and men there was very little evidence of their wanting to resume their migratory lifestyle. Some of the men, however, did say that they missed the outdoor and carefree life of constant movement but then their women preferred living the settled life of the village. Once again women helped men in making the crucial decision of altering the migratory lifestyle which had been theirs for centuries. Their hands were strengthened by the fact that as settled keepers of animals they could make a better living, both economically and in terms of the education and future of their children. The cooperative dairy of the newly-adopted village provided their animals with specially prepared feed, health care, facilities for artificial insemination, and above all a steady and good price for milk. And the rest of the compelling evidence came from their savings bank account passbooks with a steadily increasing sum which was much beyond their wildest expectations.

SOME OBSERVATIONS ON WOMEN'S ECONOMIC AND POLITICAL INVOLVEMENT

In this chapter we identified a variety of economic and political opportunities provided by milk cooperative dairying to the women of rural Gujarat. It reached a large number of segments of rural communities. Nevertheless, it left substantial portions of those communities where its help was most needed. Wherever it did, women themselves became aware of those opportunities and involved themselves in the new economic institutions and their decision-making processes. In others they had to be persuaded, targeted, and even institutionally induced to be able to play such a role. By and large their response to such opportunities was influenced and conditioned by the cultural norms of various caste and religious groups and the manner in which they had defined or carved out domains and roles for women.

Curiously enough the women at the two ends of the ethnic spectrum, i.e. those from the Brahmin families and tribal groups, displayed their eagerness to get politically involved in the new economic and political institutions.

The Brahmin women of Khadgodhara in Kaira District and of Dindoli in Surat District showed extraordinary dynamism and courage not only in involving themselves in the public life of their respective communities but they even gave a lead to the other women in doing so. Those Brahmin women leaders did not hold themselves back because of their gender. While both of them made use of the new economic institutions with an unmixed composition, their political horizons were much wider than that. They wanted to graduate from unmixed to mixed situations and also, if possible, move on to district and state level politics. Both therefore did not accept any cultural, or conventional, constraints on their access to the wider area of participatory politics. On the contrary they made use of their cultural assurance – of Brahmins as teachers, trend-setters and leaders – to build their own morale while entering an unfamiliar, and even hostile terrain.

Such a cultural recourse, for boosting one's morale, was not even needed in the case of the tribal women of Surat District for their involvement in politics. Women in tribal communities, as we saw in this chapter, did not have to contest for equal entitlements. They *had* them, and what is more, from the very start. Spontaneously and without prior effort, they showed them as shareholders, members of managing committees, and chair-women of milk cooperative societies and also of *panchayats*. They moved through the electoral ladder not as women but as members of their communities. Unlike their Brahmin counterparts, whose movement in participatory politics was an act of assertion of their gender equality, the tribal women came through the electoral mill as individuals equal to any other in their com-munity.

The respective culturally conditioned gender gaps, for the Brahmin and tribal women, were different. Since the tribal women could do pretty well most things which tribal men could do, they did not have to come out with moral and political arguments in support of their equality. As opposed to that the Brahmin women had to justify, constantly, why they were doing what they were doing.

Then there was the example of Patidar women, who came from economically and educationally more advanced groups. But such a background instead of helping their participation imposed on them additional constraints of men-defined respecta-bility. While the Patidar men were deeply involved in the participatory politics of their communities, they wanted their women to stay out of it. They even made the insulation of women from the rough and tumble of the workplace and of democratic politics a mark of their own respectability. For them political forums were not for women of good background, and the fact that their women were not required to go out to work was an indication of their economic strength. The Patidars thus manifested an extraordinary male involvement in democratic politics and a near total isolation of their women from it in rural areas. The gender gap within that community, which was otherwise at the forefront of all other socially concerned activity, was one of the greatest.

Such insulation of the Patidar women was not in evidence in urban areas, not even among those women who had recently migrated to the towns. The urban Patidar male did not equate the respectability of his family with the insulation of his women. They, on the contrary, took pride in their daughters taking a college or university education, doing a spell of work in an office before marriage, and in their wives, after the family had grown up, doing social work of some kind. Their women thus were the real beneficiaries of their migration from rural to urban areas.

The newly-acquired freedom, and expanded domain, of migratory urban Patidar women, has had a limited rub-off effect on their sisters who were left behind in rural communities. Their frequent contact changed the views of rural Patidar women towards their daughters' education, their own lifestyle, and travel. So while the older generation of Patidar women in rural areas had not much scope for a radical change in their male-dependent life, they nevertheless inadvertently allowed their own daughters to close the gap between themselves and their counterparts in urban areas.

In that respect the Chaudhury women were in a class by themselves. In the rural economy of Mehsana District they emerged as the vital resource for dairying and as keepers of milch animals. Throughout the district, and outside, the milk-producing community and the vets referred to the Chaudhury women, rather than the men, as the backbone of the milk economy. The Chaudhury women over the years had steadily built this vital role for themselves in the economy of the district. And as the milk industry acquired a prominent place in the economy so did its principal architects, the Chaudhury women. In fact no other group of women were so deeply and directly involved in the economic development of the district as the Chaudhury women. While they had played such a role for a long time, it was the emergence of the Dudhsagar Dairy which brought them into the limelight and accorded to them their due recognition.

Unlike the Brahmin and tribal women of some of the rural communities, the Chaudhury women had preferred to stay out of political institutions. While the gender distance between them and their menfolk was far narrower than among the Patidars, a caste which was pretty close to them, they preferred not to go beyond the economic domain, of both agriculture and dairying. So far as agriculture was concerned, they worked side by side with their menfolk. And in dairying, as we have already noted, they had the pre-eminent position, not only *vis-à-vis* their menfolk but also just about anybody else in the district.

After the milk strike, as we saw in this chapter, the women of the district were treated as joint, and therefore equal, members of the milk cooperative, equal owners of milch animals, and equal beneficiaries of the insurance on the life of the animal. Such a switch in the policy of Dudhsagar Dairy enormously strengthened the hands, and the confidence, of women in the district.

To that the Chaudhury women added yet another dimension to strengthen their position. Within the district, with a highly dedicated and experimenting group of brilliant veterinarians, the Chaudhury women became the first consumers of anything new that they wanted to experiment or introduce by way of cattle feed, breeding, health care, progeny testing or maintenance in general. The vets often treated them as their operational arms and display models for their new techniques and approaches. The Chaudhury women were for them the first bridge between their labs or experimental farms and the cowshed. If any of their approaches worked in the Chaudhury cowshed then the men of animal science could be certain that they would work well generally.

The Chaudhury women in the past decade had also become aware of the increasingly important role they had begun to play in the district's milk economy. That had resulted in their change of attitude to the office-holders within the milk cooperative societies. They attended meetings of the milk coop in an ever-increasing number and always had some feedback for the office-bearers, relating to their experiences or problems.

However, when it came to getting actually involved in political decision-making, they preferred to stay out of it. Often they tutored their men or even supervised them while they were speaking on their behalf with the occasional supplementary or correctional statement from the rear. But they did not want to take on the role of decision-makers by themselves. Nor did they want to engage in group politics. In fact theirs was the politics of no politics. Such a back-seat political position was as much a part of their deliberate effort to stay out of it as it was the product of their evolving social relationships with men and institutions. While their economic role had changed far more rapidly, such a fundamental change within the gender equation had yet to reflect itself fully in other relationships and in the emergence of new domains and roles for themselves.

The position of Chaudhury women could be contrasted with those of the women of Borathwada. The latter, before they were ready, and even before they had made a recognisable new contribution, were catapulted into the position of institutional decision-makers by the sheer idealism and faith of a male elite who believed that through such an elevation the traditionally disadvantaged group of women will be able to come out of their status of inequality. For their operational decisions within institutions the Borathwada women, however, always looked to and depended on male experience and confidence in running those bodies.

Their situation was similar to the average individual in India who was also elevated to the status of an electoral decision-maker when Jawaharlal Nehru, and constitutional lawyers, built free India's liberal participatory political institutions at all levels of government. They empowered the average individual with the fundamental right to choose her or his rulers within the village, subdistrict, district, state and union. Such an empowerment came very much ahead of an effective demand for it or before the average individual could build what has been already referred to as the political capacity to be able to transact her or his political business with new institutions. But once such institutions were created, and individuals empowered, the latter gradually grew in their political capacity to seek response and accountability from those officials who occupied public office.

A similar evolution of political capacity could be expected from the women of Borathwada. Now that they are in the corridors of power, they will gradually learn to function in their new role and also learn to defend their own interests.

The economic and political involvement of the women in the few communities that we examined in this chapter gave us a glimpse of its extraordinary diversity. It also indicated how very important are the cultural forces in determining the domains, roles and relationships of women with men, and of women with institutions. Above all it also pointed out how the economic and political involvements do not always occur in a sequential manner and that antecedent gender equations, cultural values, education, availability of leadership, attitudes of males towards females, and the variety of unpredictable evolutionary stages through which human social relations pass, together, make the needed difference to their gender relationships.

Notes and References

1 APPROACHES TO THE STUDY OF PROBLEMS OF WOMEN

1. See in this connection a highly perceptive collection of essays in *Defining Females: The Nature of Women in Society*, ed. Shirley Ardener (London: Croom Helm (associated with Oxford University Women's Studies Committee), 1978) p. 11. Also see *Perceiving Women*, ed. Shirley Ardener (London: J. M. Dent and Sons Limited, 1977).
2. "A Social Anthropological Approach to Women's Roles and Status in Developing Countries: The Domestic Cycle" by T. Scarlett Epstein in *Women's Roles and Population Trends in the Third World*, ed. Richard Anker, Mayra Buvinic and Nadia H. Youssef (London: Croom Helm, 1982) p. 155.
3. *Women and Space: Ground Rules and Social Maps*, ed. Shirley Ardener (London: Croom Helm, 1979) p. 11.
4. *Defining Females: The Nature of Women in Society*, p. 9.
5. See in this connection the scholarly writings of Neera Desai, in particular *The Position of Indian Women* (Bombay: Vora and Co., 1977) and *Social Change in Gujarat* (Bombay: Vora and Co., 1978).
6. Paul Thomas, *Indian Women Through the Ages* (Bombay: Asia Publishing House, 1964). Also see Charles Heimsath, *Indian Nationalism and Hindu Social Reform* (Princeton, N.J.: Princeton University Press, 1964).
7. S. Sridevi, *A Century of Indian Womanhood* (Mysore: Rao and Raghvan, 1965).
8. Margret L. Cormack, *She Who Rides a Peacock* (Bombay: Asia Publishing House, 1961) p. 105.
9. M. K. Gandhi, *Women and Social Justice* (Ahmedabad: Navjivan Publishing House, 1942).
10. *Ibid.* pp. 13–14.
11. "To the Women of India" by M. K. Gandhi in *Young India*, 1930, p. 169.
12. "Position of Women" by M. K. Gandhi in *Women and Social Justice*, p. 11.
13. Quoted by Rajkumari Amrit Kaur in her introduction to M. K. Gandhi's *Women and Social Justice*, p. 4.
14. Jawaharlal Nehru, *The Discovery of India* (Bombay: Asia Publishing House, 1967) p. 41.
15. *Ibid.* pp. 41–2.
16. Quoted by Bimla Luthra in "Nehru and the Place of Women in Indian Society" in *Indian Women: From Purdah to Modernity*, ed. B. R. Nanda (New Delhi: Vikas Publishing House, 1976) p. 3.
17. *Ibid.* p. 4.
18. *Ibid.* p. 8.
19. *Symbols of Power: Studies in Political Status of Women in India*, ed. Vina Mazumdar (Bombay: Allied Publishers, 1979) p. ix.

20. Ivan Illich, *Gender* (New York: Pantheon Books, 1982) pp. 4–5 and 127–39.

21. Ester Boserup, *Women's Role in Economic Development* (New York: St. Martin's Press, 1970) p. 5.

22. *Symbols of Power: Studies in Political Status of Women in India*, p. ix.

23. *Ibid.* p. xv.

24. See for the details of Gandhi, Nehru, JP controversy, A. H. Somjee, *Political Society in Developing Countries* (London: Macmillan, 1984) *passim* pp. 117–22.

25. Leela Gulati, *Profiles of Female Poverty: A Study of Five Poor Women of Kerala* (Delhi: Hindustan Publishing Corporation, 1981) *passim* pp. 164–7.

26. *Ibid.* p. vii.

27. "Introducing Gender Issues in Developing Countries" by Kate Young in *Seminar on Women, Work and Development: Methodological Issues, 1981–82* (New Delhi: Centre For Women's Development Studies, 1983), mimeograph, *passim* pp. 25–6.

28. "Women's Work: Major Issues" by Dr. Krishna Ahooja Patel in *Seminar on Women, Work and Development: Methodological Issues, 1981–82, passim* pp. 31–5.

29. "The Position of Women in Indian Society" by Andre Beteille in *Indian Women*, ed. Devaki Jain (New Delhi: Publication Division, Ministry of Information and Broadcasting, Government of India, 1976) pp. 22–7.

30. See in this connection *The Endless Day: Some Case Material on Asian Rural Women*, eds. T. Scarlett Epstein and Rosemary A. Watts (Oxford: Pergamon Press, 1972).

31. Barrington Moore Jr., *Social Origins of Dictatorship and Democracy* (Boston: Beacon Press, 1972).

32. Karl de Schweinitz Jr., *Industrialization and Democracy* (London: Collier-Macmillan, 1964).

33. George Lukacs, *History and Class Consciousness* (Cambridge, Mass.: MIT Press, 1976) *passim* pp. 83–110; 173–81; and 197–209.

34. *Indian Women, passim* p. xv.

35. Betty Friedan, *The Feminine Mystique* (New York: W. W. Norton and Co., 1974), and *The Second Stage* (New York: Summit Books, 1981); Germaine Greer, *The Female Eunuch* (London: MacGibbon and Kee, 1970) and *Sex and Destiny* (London: Secker and Warburg, 1984).

36. For an extended analysis of the concept of political capacity see A. H. Somjee, *Political Capacity in Developing Societies*, pp. 17–28.

2   URBAN WOMEN: THE TWO GENERATIONS

1. Karl Mannheim, *Essays on the Sociology of Knowledge* (London: Routledge and Kegan Paul, 1952). See the section on "The Problem of Generations", pp. 282–90.

2. A. H. Somjee, *The Democratic Process in a Developing Society* (London: Macmillan, 1979).

3. Ester Boserup, *Women's Role in Economic Development* (New York: St. Martin's Press, 1970).
4. *Ibid.* p. 159.
5. *Ibid.* p. 159.
6. "From Purdah to Modernity" by Rama Mehta in *Indian Women: From Purdah to Modernity*, ed. B. R. Nanda (New Delhi: Vikas Publishing House, 1976).
7. Rhoda L. Goldstein, *Indian Women in Transition: A Bangalore Case Study* (Metuchen, N.J.: The Scarecrow Press, 1972) p. 75.
8. Promila Kapur, *The Changing Status of Working Women in India* (New Delhi: Vikas Publishing House, 1974) p. viii.
9. *Ibid.* p. 17.
10. *Ibid.* p. 22.
11. Rama Mehta, *The Western Educated Woman*, p. 37.
12. *Ibid.* p. 152.
13. David Pocock, *Kanbi and Patidar: A Study of a Patidar Community of Gujarat* (Oxford: Oxford University Press, 1972) p. 156.
14. "The Hypergamy of the Patidars" by David Pocock in *Professor Ghurye Felicitation Volume* (Bombay: Popular Book Depot, 1954) p. 198.
15. "Social Mobility Among the Patidars of Kaira" by A. H. Somjee in *Contributions to Asian Studies*, Vol. 12, 1978, pp. 105–13.
16. See in this connection my paper on "Social Change in Nursing Profession in India" in *The Anthropology of Nursing*, ed. Pat Holden (London: Croom Helm, 1988).

3 URBAN ELITES AND THE REGENERATIVE PROCESSES

1. C. Balaji and P. Durgaprasad, *A Study in Cooperative Dairy Education and Development Programme For Women* (Anand: Institute of Rural Management, 1985) p. 16.
2. *Ibid.* p. 19.
3. *Ibid.* p. 39.
4. See *The Annual Report of Tribhuvandas Foundation, 1983–84* (Gamadi, Anand: Anand Press, 1984).
5. *Ibid. passim* pp. 2–9.
6. Earlier, Drs R. and M. Arole had jointly worked in a village called Jamkhed in Maharastra state towards the organisation of a successful Comprehensive Rural Health Project which later on became a source of inspiration to the National Dairy Development Board in its attempt to have its own health programme in Kaira district. This programme was implemented by the Tribhuvandas Foundation. See in this connection the *Anand Pattern Integrated Rural Development Programme* (Anand: NDDB, 1979).
7. *The Annual Report of the Tribhuvandas Foundation*, 1983–4, p. 9.
8. Data for this was collected in 1982, 1983, 1984, 1985, 1986 and 1987 by means of repeated interviews.

9. See for the details of the activity of SEWA, Jennefer Sebstad's *Struggle and Development Among Self-Employed Women: A Report on the Self-Employed Women's Association, Ahmedabad, India* (Washington, D.C.: Office of Urban Development Bureau for Development Support Agency for International Development, 1982).

10. *Ibid.* p. 220.

11. *Ibid.* pp. 17–18.

12. *Ibid.* p. 219.

13. See in this connection *Indian and Foreign Review*, Vol. 21, No. 21, 1984, pp. 24–5.

14. *We, the Self-Employed* (Ahmedabad: SEWA Reception Centre, 1982) p. 5.

15. *Ibid.* p. 5.

16. "Experiences with Rural Women" and "Jaago Project: The Second Phase" by Anila R. Dholakia (Ahmedabad: SEWA Publications, 1983).

17. See in this connection, "SEWA's Women's Dairy Cooperatives: A Case Study from Gujarat" by Marty Chen and Anila Dholakia in *Indian Women: A Study of their Role in the Dairy Movement*, eds. Marty Chen, Manoshi Mitra *et al.* (New Delhi: Shakti Books, 1986) pp. 70–106.

18. See for the details of such constraints in India, and in other countries, A. H. Somjee, *Political Capacity in Devleoping Societies* (London: Macmillan, 1982).

19. "Peasant Movement: Women and Rural Revolt in India" by Gail Omvedt in *The Journal of Peasant Studies*, Vol. 5, 1978.

4 ASPECTS OF ECONOMIC AND POLITICAL INVOLVEMENT IN RURAL COMMUNITIES

1. See for the details of this "DUDHSAGAR Dairy: A Cooperative Miracle in an Arid Land" by Geeta Somjee and A. H. Somjee in *The Journal of Development Studies*, 1986.

2. For a detailed study of this see G. S. Ghurye, *The Scheduled Tribes* (Bombay: Popular Prakashan, 1963).

3. *Service Centres Planning in Tribal areas of Gujarat State*, ed. Shankar Gohil (Ahmedabad: Gujarat Institute of Area Planning, 1982).

4. Data collected by means of repeated interviews at the village level as well as at Sumul headquarters in Surat.

5. Ghanshyam Shah and H. R. Chaturvedi, *Gandhian Approach to Rural Development: the Valod Experiment* (New Delhi: Ajanta Publications, 1983) pp. 85–95.

6. See for the details of this "Cooperative Dairying and the Profiles of Social Change in India" by A. H. Somjee and Geeta Somjee, *Economic Development and Cultural Change*, 1978.

Index